Making Out in Hindi

Making Out in Hindi

Daniel Krasa & Rainer Krack

with the invaluable assistance of Rajneesh Mangla

TUTTLE Publishing

Tokyo | Rutland, Vermont | Singapore

Published by Tuttle Publishing, an imprint of Periplus Editions (HK) Ltd.

www.tuttlepublishing.com

Illustrations by Kathy Sugianto

Library of Congress Cataloging-in-Publication Data
Krasa, Daniel.
Making out in Hindi / Daniel Krasa & Rainer Krack.
p. cm.
Text in English and Hindi.
ISBN 978-0-8048-4167-2 (pbk.)
1. Hindi language--Conversation and phrase books--English. I. Krack, Rainer. II. Title.
PK1935.K73 2011
491.4'383421--dc22

2011000105

ISBN 978-0-8048-4167-2

Distributed by

North America, Latin America & Europe
Tuttle Publishing
364 Innovation Drive
North Clarendon, VT 05759-9436 U.S.A.
Tel: 1 (802) 773-8930
Fax: 1 (802) 773-6993
info@tuttlepublishing.com
www.tuttlepublishing.com

Asia-Pacific
Berkeley Books Pte. Ltd.
61 Tai Seng Avenue #02-12
Singapore 534167
Tel: (65) 6280-1330
Fax: (65) 6280-6290
inquiries@periplus.com.sg
www.periplus.com

First edition
15 14 13 12 11 1106CP
8 7 6 5 4 3 2

Printed in Singapore

Contents

Pronunciation Guide

Nothing beats listening to a native speaker, but the following notes should help you to attain the right pronunciation. The Hindi transcription used in this book is the internationally most common one. English speakers must pay attention to some main differences in order to make themselves understood. Here are the basic rules:

VOWELS

Most vowels in Hindi have a clear equivalent in English, so that pronouncing should not pose any major problem.

The vowels are:

Hindi letter		*Approximate English equivalent*
अ	**a**	**run, fun**; sometimes, when between a consonant and h, as in **bad**
आ	**ā**	**father**, *as in Southern British*
ऐ	**ai**	**lie**
औ	**au**	**couch**
ए	**e**	*between* **best** *and* **paid**
इ	**i**	**hit**
ई	**ī**	**heat**
ओ	**o**	*between Southern British* **cot** *and* **door**
उ	**u**	**put**
ऊ	**ū**	**moon**

The Hindi vowels differ in length—as in **shabd** (word) and **āj** (today). But there is a degree of variation in the pronunciation of certain vowels, often due to regional differences.

Consonants

Unlike the Hindi vowel system, the consonants are more complex and to master them some more information is necessary:

Retroflex consonants

There is a crucial difference between dental and retroflex consonants in Hindi. In dental consonants, the tongue touches the upper front teeth, whereas retroflex consonants are pronounced with the tongue turned back to the roof of your mouth. For example, set your mouth up to pronounce a "regular" d, but then curl your tongue right up so that the bottom part of it touches the top part of your mouth. As you try to pronounce the original d, you will feel your tongue "flapping" forward. American English has also some of these retroflex sounds, most commonly in the middle of words like "bidder", "heart", and "bitter", or at the end of words like "bad", "butter", and "bat". The three retroflex consonants are: **ḍ**, **ṭ**, and **ṇ**. Strictly speaking **ṣ** is also a retroflex, but in practice it is rarely distinguished from an English "sh".

Aspirated consonants

Hindi also distinguishes breathed or aspirated consonants from light or non-aspirated ones. Aspirated consonants are those pronounced with an audible expulsion of breath, i.e. a discernable, heavy puff of air. The aspirated consonants are marked by an h following them (except for sh which is always pronounced as the English "sh") and they are: **bh, ch, dh, ḍh, gh, jh, kh, ph, th** and **ṭh**.

On the other hand, non-aspirated consonants are pronounced far lighter—i.e. with minimal breath—than their English equivalents. For the matter of making yourself understand it is vital to emphasize the difference between aspirated and unaspirated consonants.

Nasalization

Hindi has several nasal consonants which affect the vowel placed before them in a similar way to the "n" in French (e.g. "bon") or the Portuguese "m" (e.g. "bem"). These nasal sounds are: **ṃ**, **ñ** and **ṅ** but even the consonants **m**, **n** and **ṇ** can cause light nasalization when positioned in front of another consonant, e.g. **Mumbaī** (Mumbai)

The consonants are:

Hindi letter		*Approximate English equivalent*
ब	**b**	box, "*light*"
भ	**bh**	box, "*breathed*"
च	**c**	champion
छ	**ch**	church, "*breathed*"
द	**d**	dog, "*light*"
ध	**dh**	dog, "*breathed*"
ड	**ḍ**	like **d**, "*flapped*"—*in the middle of a word often like a "flapped" r*
ढ	**ḍh**	like **ḍ**, "*breathed*"
फ़	**f**	fat
ग	**g**	give, "*light*"

Note: In Arabic and Persian loanwords the **g** sound is sometimes produced further back against the epiglottis, and is in those cases underlined: **g̲**. However not all speakers of Hindi use this sound and **g̲** may thus be rendered as **g** at all times. The difference in sound is minute and can only be detected by advanced speakers. The **g̲** sounds a tiny bit "scratchy".

घ	**gh**	give, "*breathed*"
ह	**h**	hat
ज	**j**	jet, "*light*"
झ	**jh**	jet, "*breathed*"
क / क़	**k**	kick, "*light*"

Note: As with g, in Arabic and Persian loanwords the k sound is sometimes produced against the epiglottis, and in those cases is underlined: **<u>k</u>**.

ख / ख़	**kh**	kick, "*breathed*"

Note: In Arabic and Persian loanwords kh is sometimes pronounced as the **ch** in Scottish lo**ch**—in this case we underline it: **<u>kh</u>**—however not all speakers of Hindi use this sound and **<u>kh</u>** may thus be rendered as **kh** at all times.

ल	**l**	let
म	**m**	mat
	ṃ	like **m**, "*lightly nasalized*"
न	**n**	need
ण	**ṇ**	like **n**, "*flapped*"
	ñ	like **n**, "*nasalized*"
	n˙	ink
प	**p**	pet, "*light*"
फ	**ph**	pet, "*breathed*"
र	**r**	rat, *but rolled as in Scottish English or Italian*
	ṛ	"*flapped*" *r as in the American* butter
स	**s**	sit
श	**sh**	shine
ष	**ṣ**	like **s**, "*flapped*"*—but most often pronounced* like **sh**
त	**t**	**ten**, "*light*"
थ	**th**	ten, "*breathed*"
ट	**ṭ**	like **t**, "*flapped*"
ठ	**ṭh**	like **ṭ**, "*breathed*"
व	**v**	way
ज़	**z**	zebra, "*light*"

English loan words

Note that there are numerous English loan words in Hindi and they are generously used in casual conversation. These loan words get the Great Indian Masala Treatment, craftily adjusting them to local tongues and ears. The result may at first be unintelligible to native English speakers. It will take time (or **ṭāim**, as Hindi speakers would say) to get used to the Indianized pronunciation.

The consonants **t** and **d** are usually pronounced like the retroflex consonants **ṭ** and **ḍ** (see **ṭāim**), and **o** sometimes becomes a slightly nasalized **a** or **ā** (as in **prāblam** = problem, **affis** = office, **lāṭ** = lord, the latter being hardly recognizable from the original).

Synonyms

The Hindi vocabulary is augmented by many words from non-Indian languages (mostly Persian and Arabic), and consequently, there are often several synonyms for any one word in English. As we will see, there are five synonyms for the humble word "but"; some are derived from Sanskrit, others from foreign sources. There are also five Hindi words for "blood" (**khūn, rakt, rudhir, lahū, lohu**). It is advisable to memorize all the synonyms that will crop up in the course of our little book: Regionally and individually a different synonym may be preferred—and you wouldn't want to get stuck because of that silly fifth word for "but", would you?

Hindi loan words in English

Languages don't just travel on one-way streets: During the time of the British Raj, the British colonial period in India, the foreign rulers imported many words from Indian languages. Some were corrupted beyond recognition, but "something is better than nothing", as the Indians say. Here are a few of the most common words taken from Hindi:

- Bandanna (from **bāndhnā**, to bind)
- Bungalow (from **baṅglā**, a one-storeyed house)
- Cha (from **cāy**, tea; the basis of the quaint old Briticism "Fancy a cuppa cha, my dear?")
- Curry (from **kaṛhī**, a spicy sauce or soup)
- Dacoit (from **ḍākū**, robber)
- Juggernaut (from **Jagannāth**, another name for God Vishnu)
- Jungle (from **jaṅgal**, a thick forest or wasteland)
- Maharaja (from **mahārājā**, great king)
- Mahout (from **mahāvaṭ**, a keeper or driver of elephants)
- Pyjamas (from **pājāmā**, a kind of loose cotton pants)
- Punch (the drink), from **pāñc** (five), since the original beverage was concocted from five ingredients
- Shampoo (from **campī**, a head massage, and **cāmpnā**, to massage)
- Thug (from **ṭhag**, deceiver; also the word for a member of a murderous cult called **ṭhagī**, whose adherents roamed the Indian countryside and robbed and killed travelers in the name of Goddess Kali.)
- To loot (from **lūṭnā**, to rob, plunder)
- Verandah (from **baraṇḍā**)

Pronunciation, the pitfalls

As we have seen, there are different kinds of consonants in Hindi ("regular" and retroflex, aspirated and unaspirated), as well as different kinds of vowels (long and short). To the untrained ear, the difference may appear minor, but employing the wrong type of consonant or wrong length of vowel can fatally alter the meaning of a word. For example:
ḍāl = a lentil dish; **dal** = group, team, (political) party.
nāṭā = small in stature; **nātā** = relationship.

Pronunciation, some encouragement

Initially, pronouncing a new language might get your tongue in a proverbial twist, but practice makes perfect—so don't be shy at speaking, even at the risk of making mistakes or gaffes. There are only a few non-Indian Hindi speakers, and the locals will be absolutely delighted to find a foreigner making the effort to learn their mother tongue. They will gladly help you improve your skills. Simply go for it!

The Hindi alphabet

Hindi letter	*Roman equivalent*	*Hindi Letter*	*Roman equivalent*
अ	**a**	ण	**ṇ**
आ	**ā**	त	**t**
इ	**i**	थ	**th**
ई	**ī**	द	**d**
उ	**u**	ध	**dh**
ऊ	**ū**	न	**n**
ऋ	**ri**	प	**p**
ए	**e**	फ / फ़	**ph/f**
ऐ	**ai**	ब	**b**
ओ	**o**	भ	**bh**
औ	**au**	म	**m**
क / क़	**k/<u>k</u>**	य	**y**
ख / ख़	**kh/<u>kh</u>**	र	**r**
ग	**g**	ल	**l**
घ	**gh**	व	**v**
च	**c**	श	**sh**
छ	**ch**	ष	**ṣ**
ज / ज़	**j/z**	स	**s**
झ	**jh**	ह	**h**
ट	**ṭ**		
ठ	**ṭh**	क्ष	**kṣ**
ड	**ḍ**	ज्ञ	**jny**
ढ	**ḍh**		

The full forms of the vowels are written at the beginning or end of a word, or when they are in combination with another vowel. Otherwise Hindi writes the vowels with small signs over, under, before or after the consonant that comes before them.

A TINY BIT OF GRAMMAR

The old sex thing

We knew that this would get your attention, so let's talk about ...well, actually, gender. In Hindi grammar there are two genders, male and female. Nouns have either male or female gender and any adjective relating to a noun has to adjust its gender to the gender of the noun—somewhat like in French. Verbs also have male and female forms. Depending on who is acting, the verb will have to adopt the male form ♂ or female ♀ form.

What's Your Address?

Nope, we're not gonna write you a letter. It's all about addressing people. There are three types of addresses in Hindi, three words for the simple English "you". Which of the three you use depends on your relationship with, or the status of, the person you wish to address.

- **tū** – OK among very close relatives, friends and lovers, otherwise it's insulting. It's sometimes deliberately used to demean someome.
- **tum** – Used among friends, family members and good acquaintances.
- **āp** – the most polite form of address, for people of high standing, strangers, and in formal situations.

Similarly, the possessive pronoun "your" has three forms: **terā/terī**, **tumhārā/tumhārī** and **āpkā/āpkī**. Grammatically, the pronouns are treated like adjectives, so their gender would have to be adjusted to the gender of the associated noun.

What's Up? 1

Good morning/ afternoon/evening!	Namaskār! नमस्कार !

Note: Unlike English, Hindi has different forms of greeting depending on the speaker's religion. Hindus use **Namaskār!**, **Namaste!** or **Rām rām!**, Sikhs use **Sat srī akāl!** and Muslims greet each other with **Salām alaikum!**.

How are you?	Āp kaise♂/kaisī♀ haiñ? आप कैसे/कैसी हैं ?
How are you doing?	Āpkā hāl kyā hai? आपका हाल क्या है ?
I'm fine. And you?	Maiñ ṭhīk hūñ. Aur āp? मैं ठीक हूँ । और आप ?
Do you remember/ recognize me?	Mujhe pahcānte ho? मुझे पहचानते हो ?

Casual greetings between friends

Hello!	Hello! हेलो !
How are you?	Tum kaise♂/kaisī♀ ho? तुम कैसे/कैसी हो ?
How's things with you?	Kyā hāl–cāl hai? क्या हाल-चाल है ?
I'm fine.	Maiñ ṭhīk hūñ. मैं ठीक हूँ ।

What's up?	Kyā <u>kh</u>abar? क्या ख़बर ?
What's the news?	Kyā samācār? क्या समाचार ?

So-so.	Ṭhīk-ṭhāk. ठीक-ठाक।
Everything's alright.	Sab ṭhīk-ṭhāk. सब ठीक-ठाक।
Not very well.	Kāfī acchā ♂/acchī ♀ nahīñ. काफ़ी अच्छा/अच्छी नहीं।
Not bad.	Koī taklīf nahīñ. कोई तकलीफ़ है।
What's new?	Kyā naī bāt hai? क्या नई बात है ?
Nothing much.	Kuch <u>kh</u>ās nahīñ. कुछ ख़ास नहीं।

Everything as usual.	Sab aisā–vaisā. सब ऐसा-वैसा ।

Speakers with a bit of a poetic bent may say: **Are, vohī din, vohī rāteñ** ... = "Alas, it's the same (old) days, the same (old) nights ...".

How have you been?	Tum kaise rahe ♂/ kaisī rahīñ ♀? तुम कैसे रहे/कैसी रहीं ?
I've been fine, thank you.	Maiñ ṭhīk rahā ♂/ rahī ♀, shukriyā. मैं ठीक रहा/रही, शुक्रिया ।
Long time no see!	Itnī der ke bād! इतनी देर के बाद !

Literally "After such a long time (do we meet again)!"

What have you been up to?	Tum kyā kar rahe the ♂/ rahī thīñ ♀? तुम क्या कर रहे थे/रही थीं ?
I'm pretty busy.	Maiñ ekdam *busy* hūñ. मैं एकदम बिज़ी हूँ ।
Do you live around here?	Tum yahāñ bas rahe ♂/ rahī ♀ ho? तुम यहाँ बस रहे/रही हो ?
Are you staying around here?	Tum yahāñ hī rahte ♂/ rahtī ♀ ho? तुम यहाँ ही रहते/रहती हो ?
Yes, I live here.	Hāñ, maiñ yahāñ hī rahtā ♂/ rahtī ♀ hūñ. हाँ, मैं यहाँ ही रहता/रहती हूँ ।
Where do you live?	Tum kahāñ rahte ♂/ rahtī ♀ ho? तुम कहाँ रहते/रहती हो ?

Where are you staying?	Tum kahāñ ṭhaharte ♂/ ṭhahartī ♀ ho? तुम कहाँ ठहरते/ठहरती हो ?
I haven't seen you around for a while.	Maiñ ne tum ko bahut ṭāim se dekhā nahīñ. मैं ने तुम को बहुत टाइम से देखा नहीं ।

Note: Several pronouns in the dative and accusative case have two forms in Hindi. Both **mujhe** and **mujhko** "me" or **tum ko** and **tumheñ** "you" can be used equally.

Yes, it's been a long time.	Hāñ, bahut ṭāim ke bād. हाँ, बहुत टाइम के बाद ।
Why don't you show up sometimes?	Kyoñ dikhāī nahīñ de rahe ♂/ rahī ♀ ho? क्यों दिखाई नहीं दे रहे/रही हो ?
What are you doing here?	Tum yahāñ kyā kar rahe ♂/ rahī ♀ ho? तुम यहाँ क्या कर रहे/रही हो ?
How's Peter/ Mary doing?	Peter/Mary kā hāl kyā hai? पीटर/मैरी का हाल क्या है ?
He's/She's fine.	Acchā ♂/Acchī ♀ hai. अच्छा/अच्छी है ।
OK, take care!	Ṭhīk hai, apnā <u>kh</u>ayāl rakhnā! ठीक है, अपना ख़याल रखना !
What's the problem?	Kyā taklīf hai? क्या तकलीफ़ है ?
What happened?	Kyā huā? क्या हुआ ?
What's on your mind?	Kyā soc rahe ♂/rahī ♀ ho? क्या सोच रहे/रही हो ?

Nothing.	Kuch nahīñ. कुछ नहीं ।
I was just thinking.	Maiñ sirf soc rahā thā♂/ rahī thī♀. मैं सिर्फ़ सोच रहा था/रही थी ।
Is this any of your business!	Tumhārā yah sab kyā hai? तुम्हारा यह सब क्या है ?
Keep out of this!	Hastakṣep mat karo! हस्तक्षेप मत करो !
Leave me alone!	Mujhe choṛ do! मुझे छोड़ दो !
Leave it!/Let it rest!	Choṛ do! छोड़ दो !
Get lost!	Bhāgo! भागो!
Back off!	Haṭ! हट !
Go away!	Calo yahāñ se! चलो यहाँ से !
Don't show up again!	Phir dikhāī mat denā! फिर दिखाई मत देना !
Really?	Sac? सच ?
Is that so?	Aisā hotā hai? ऐसा होता है ?
That's correct, isn't it?	Barābar hai, na? बराबर है, न ?
Is that correct?	Barābar hai, kyā? बराबर है, क्या ?

Oh yeah?	Acchā? अच्छा ?
Lies!	Jhūṭ! झूट !
You're lying.	Tum jhūṭ bol rahe ♂/ rahī ♀ ho. तुम झूट बोल रहे/रही हो ।
Don't lie!	Jhūṭ mat bolo! झूट मत बोलो !
Don't talk nonsense!	Bako mat! बको मत !

Note: Alternatively, one could say **Bakvās mat karo!**, but this could also mean "Don't do anything stupid", "Don't make that nonsense/nuisance!" etc.

How come?	Yah kaise? यह कैसे ?
What are you saying/ what do you mean?	Kyā bol rahe ♂/rahī ♀ ho? क्या बोल रहे/रही हो ?
You don't say so!	Bolo mat! बोलो मत !

An exclamation meaning "This can't be true!" Another version is **Are bāp!** अरे बाप ! (An exclamation of surprise translating closer to "Oh my dear!")

Don't say that!	Aisā mat bolo! ऐसा मत बोलो !
Is something wrong?	Kuch galat huā? कुछ ग़लत हुआ ?
What?	Kyā? क्या ?

Huh?	Kyā? क्या ?
Say that again!	Dubārā bol! दुबारा बोल !

Note that this can come across as aggressive, like an invitation to a fight, verbal or otherwise. If you didn't catch what the other person said, better remain polite and say **kripayā dubārā boli(y)e!** = would you say that again, please!

Are you serious?	Sahī bāt hai, kyā? सही बात है, क्या ?
Is that so?	Sac hai, kyā? सच है, कया ?

If you feel a bit lazy, you could simply ask **saccī**? "true?", which is an abbreviated, colloquial from of **saccī bāt**? "true speech?".

Tell me why!	Batāo kyoñ! बताओ क्यों !
It is true.	Yah sac hai. यह सच है !
That's impossible!	Yah na-mumkin hai! यह न-मुमकिन है !
Enough!	Bas! बस !
What a mess!	Kyā gaṛbaṛ hai! क्या गड़बड़ है !
What nonsense!	Kyā bakvās hai! क्या बकवास है !
How crazy!	Kyā pāgalpan! क्या पागलपन
You're crazy!	Tum pāgal ho! तुम पागल हो !

What's all this commotion?	Yah kyā tamāshā ho gayā? यह क्या तमाशा हो गया ?

Note: Yah kyā tamāshā ho gayā? literally means "What kind of show is this?" and is used when something is out of control.

I don't believe it!	Yah maiñ nahīñ māntā♂/ māntī♀. यह मैं नहीं मानता/मानती ।
You're joking!	Tum mazāk̲ uṛā rahe♂/ rahī♀ ho! तुम मज़ाक़ उड़ा रहे/रही हो !
Are you pulling my leg?	Merā mazāk̲ uṛā rahe♂/ rahī♀ ho? मेरा मज़ाक़ उड़ा रहे/रही हो ?
Are you making a fool of me?	Mujhe ullū banā rahe♂/ rahī♀ ho? मुझे उल्लू बना रहे/रही हो ?

Note: Literally "Are you turning me into an owl?" Unlike in Western fables, in India, the owl is considered a bit of a dimwit. "To be an owl" is equivalent to being a fool, simpleton. **Ullū kā paṭṭhā** = a still young, but fully-grown offspring of an owl = clumsy fool. In the above sentence, you could replace **ullū** with **bakrā** "goat". **Kisī ko bakrā banānā** "to turn someone into a goat" = to fool someone, to trick someone.

Stop joking!	Bas, mazāk̲ mat uṛāo! बस, मज़ाक़ मत उड़ाओ !
I'm not joking!	Maiñ mazāk̲ nahīñ uṛā rahā♂/ rahī♀ hūñ! मैं मज़ाक़ नहीं उड़ा रहा/रही हूँ !
That's right!	Sahī bāt hai! सही बात है !
Absolutely!	Bilkul! बिलकुल !

Definitely!	Pakkā! पक्का !
Without a doubt!	Beshak! बेशक !
Of course!	Zarūr! ज़रूर !
I'm telling the truth!	Maiñ sac hī bol rahā ♂/ rahī ♀ hūñ! मैं सच ही बोल रहा/रही हूँ !
No way!	Nahīñ re! नहीं रे !
Never!	Kabhī nahīñ! कभी नहीं !
I guess so.	Andāz hai. अंदाज़ है ।
I think so.	Mujhe aisā lagtā hai. मुझे ऐसा लगता है ।
I hope so.	Mujhe ummīd hai. मुझे उम्मीद है ।
I hope not.	Mujhe ummīd nahīñ. मुझे उम्मीद नहीं ।
I doubt it.	Shak hai. शक है ।
I don't think so.	Mujhe aisā nahīñ lagtā. मुझे ऐसा नहीं लगता ।
I'm not sure.	Mujhe ṭhīk se patā nahīñ. मुझे ठीक से पता नहीं ।
God knows	Rām jāne. राम जाने ।

Note: **Rām jāne.** is only used by Hindus.

God willing!	Bhagvān agar cāhā! भगवान अगर चाहा !

Note: Muslims would rather say **inshāllāh!**, which can also mean "From your mouth to God's ear!"

No idea ...	Patā nahīñ... पता नहीं ...
What do I know!	Kyā patā! क्या पता !
What the hell do I know!	Sālā, mujhe kyā patā! साला, मुझे क्या पता !

Note: Due to the **sālā** (see page 84) this is somewhat rude, so don't use it lightly.

What do I care!	Mujhe kyā parvāh! मुझे क्या परवाह !
Forget it!	Bhūl jāo! भूल जाओ !
Let it be!	Rahne do! रहने दो !
Damn!	Abe! अबे !

Mind, this should not be pronounced like the good old All-American name Abe. The "e" sounds a bit like a French é (think café) and in this case it's also strongly stressed: **a-bé!** The more stress you put on it, the more powerful the curse!

Bullshit, man!	Bakvās, yār! बकवास, यार !
Don't do that!	Aisā mat karo! ऐसा मत करो !
Don't you dare!/ Watch out!	<u>Kh</u>abardār! ख़बरदार !

How dare you!
Tumhārī yahī himmat?
तुम्हारी यही हिम्मत ?

Hindi speakers would turn this sentence into a question, literally asking "You have this here courage?" (as to do a certain thing).

Not my business!
Merā koī len-den nahīñ!
मेरा कोई लेन-देन नहीं !

That's none of my business.
Merā us se koī len-den nahīñ.
मेरा उस से कोई लेन-देन नहीं !

So what?
To, phir?
तो, फिर ?

What else?/What next?
Aur kyā?
और क्या ?

Aur kyā can also be used as an exclamation instead of a question —in the sense of "Of course, what do you think!" For example: Have you eaten the whole cake by yourself? Answer: **Aur kyā!** = Of course I have! Did you think I wouldn't? Ha!

What now?/What next?
Āge kyā hogā?
आगे क्या होगा ?

It means nothing to me.
Yah mere li(y)e kuch nahīñ.
यह मेरे लिए कुछ नहीं ।

I'm not interested.
Is meñ koī shauk nahīñ.
इस में कोई शौक़ नहीं ।

Sure, if you like.
Hāñ, agar tum ko cāhie.
हाँ, अगर तुम को चाहिए ।

Whatever you want.
Jo tum ko cāhie.
जो तुम को चाहिए ।

As you wish.
Tumhārī marzī.
तुम्हारी मरज़ी ।

What do you think?
Tum ko kyā lagtā hai?
तुम को क्या लगता है ?

I think so, too.	Mujhe bhī aisā lagtā hai. मुझे भी ऐसा लगता है ।
So am I.	Maiñ bhī. मैं भी ।
Me too.	Mujhe bhī. मुझे भी ।
Got it! Understood!	Samjhā♂/samjhī♀! समझा/समझी !
I see what you mean.	Tumhārī bāteñ samajh meñ āyīñ. तुम्हारी बातें समझ में आयीं ।
OK, that's good enough!	Ṭhīk hai, calegā! ठीक है, चलेगा !
OK, this is enough.	Ṭhīk hai, itnā hī calegā. ठीक है, इतना ही चलेगा ।
Great!	Baṛhiyā! बढ़िया !

Note: You might also hear **bhārī**, **bindās**, **dhāsū**, **faṇḍū**, **jhakās**, **kamāl** or **mast**, however these words are rather colloquial and used only regionally and/or among the very young.

Well done!/Bravo! Shabāsh!
शबाश !

Wow! Vāh!
वाह !

Not bad! Burā nahīñ!
बुरा नहीं !

I like it! Mujhe pasand hai!
मुझे पसंद है !

I don't like it! Mujhe pasand nahīñ!
मुझे पसंद नहीं !

That was great!/ I liked it! Mujhe pasand āyā!
मुझे पसंद आया !

No problem! Koī mushkil/prāblam nahīñ!
कोई मुश्किल/प्रॉबलम नहीं !

Note that the English word "problem" is curiously popular in India and it is frequently used in Hindi speech. Its pronunciation, though, is "Hindi-ised" and it may not be immediately recognizable to native English speakers.

It's no problem! Is meñ koī mushkil/prāblam nahīñ!
इस में कोई मुश्किल/प्रॉबलम नहीं!

But... Magar/Lekin...
मगर/लेकिन...

As mentioned earlier, Hindi boasts five synonyms for the simple English word "but": **magar, lekin, par, parantu** and **kintu**. The first two are very common; the third a bit less so. **Parantu** and **kintu** sound quite formal or stiff, but they are sometimes used tongue-in-cheek, in a kind of mock hi-falutin' way.

Cheer up! Prasann ho!
प्रसन्न हो !

You look happy.	Tum <u>kh</u>ush lag rahe♂/ rahī♀ ho. तुम खुश लग रहे/रही हो।
You look troubled.	Tum pareshān lag rahe♂/ rahī♀ ho. तुम परेशान लग रहे/रही हो।
You look sad.	Tum udās lag rahe♂/ rahī♀ ho. तुम उदास लग रहे/रही हो।
Slowly!	Dhīre-dhīre! धीरे-धीरे !
Slowly!/Carefully!	Āhistā-āhistā! आहिस्ता- आहिस्ता !
Take it easy!/Relax!	Ārām karo! आराम करो !
Don't worry!	Fi<u>k</u>r/cintā mat karo! फ़िक्र/चिंता मत करो !
Never mind!	Koī bāt nahīñ! कोई बात नहीं !

Note: Koī bāt nahīñ! can also mean "It doesn't matter."

Have fun!	Mazā/aish karo! मज़ा/ऐश करो !
Rock on!	Lage raho! लगे रहो !

Literally "Carry on!" If you get the chance, watch the 2006 cult movie *Lage Raho Munna Bhai!* (*Carry on, Munna Bhai!*) with Sanjay Dutt in the title role. It's about a lovable rogue who changes from no-gooder into the epitome of the Gandhian idealist. The movie sparked a minor Gandhi revival in India and turned Dutt into a mega-star. Keep your ears well-pricked, as the dialogues are peppered with plenty of hip Mumbai street lingo.

Good luck! Shubhkāmnāeñ!
शुभकामनाएं !

Also quite common: the "Hinglish" version **guḍ lak!** "good luck!".

Have a good trip. Tumhārī yātrā maṅgalmay ho!
तुम्हारी यात्रा मंगलमय हो !

Note: Tumhārī yātrā maṅgalmay ho! might seem too formal among friends, a good alternative is either **Safar mubārak ho!** or simply "Happy journey!"

Goodbye, see you again! Phir mileñge!
फिर मिलेंगे !

Take good care of yourself! Backe rahnā!
बचके रहना !

Literally "Stay saved!"

Yes and No/ Basic Phrases

2

Yes	Hāñ हाँ
Yes, Sir/Madam (polite)	Jī hāñ जी हाँ
No	Nahīñ नहीं
No, Sir/Madam (polite)	Jī nahīñ जी नहीं
Okay	Ṭhīk hai ठीक है
What?	Kyā? क्या ?
Who?	Kaun? कौन ?
Who's that?	Yah kaun hai? यह कौन है ?
Who is it?	Kaun hai? कौन है ?
Who's there?	Vahāñ kaun hai? वहाँ कौन है ?

Whose?	Kiskā♂?/Kiskī♀? किसका?/किसकी?

Note that the gender used depends on the gender of the substantive that follows (see above). For example: **Kiskā māl?** "Whose stuff?", but **Kiskī gāṛī?** "Whose car?" For a beginner, though, it's OK to always use the male form **Kiskā?**—it's not a major gaffe in casual speech.

Where?	Kahāñ?/Kidhar? कहाँ ?/किधर ?
Where to?	Kahāñ?/Kidhar? कहाँ ?/किधर ?
Where is ...	... kahāñ hai? ... कहाँ है ?
Where are you going?	Kahāñ jā rahe♂/rahī♀ ho? कहाँ जा रहे/रही हो ?
Which country are you from?	Āpkā mulk kaunsā hai? आपका मुल्क कौनसा है ?
When?	Kab? कब ?
When (exactly)?	Kabhī? कभी ?
Why?	Kyoñ? क्यों ?
Why not?	Kyoñ nahīñ? क्यों नहीं ?
Because...	Kyoñki... क्योंकि ...
How?	Kaise? कैसे ?

Which one?	Kaunsā ♂?/Kaunsī ♀? कौनसा ?/कौनसी ?

Note: Again, the gender used depends on the gender of the associated noun. For example: **Kaunsā ādmī?** "Which man?", but **Kaunsī aurat?** "Which woman?".

Which ones?	Kaunse ♂?/Kaunsī ♀? कौनसे ?/कौनसी ?
This.	Yah. यह ।
That.	Vah. वह ।
This here.	Yahī. यही ।
That there.	Vahī. वही ।
Here.	Yahāñ. यहाँ ।
Over here.	Yahāñ hī. यहाँ ही ।
There.	Vahāñ. वहाँ ।
Over there.	Vahāñ hī. वहाँ ही ।
Somewhere.	Kahīñ. कहीं ।
Anywhere.	Kahīñ bhī. कहीं भी ।
Nowhere.	Kahīñ nahīñ. कहीं नहीं ।

Everywhere.	Har jagah. हर जगह ।
Maybe.	Shāyad. शायद ।
Maybe not.	Shāyad nahīñ. शायद नहीं ।
I	Maiñ मैं
You	Tū तू

(among close friends and relatives; otherwise impolite)

Tum
तुम

(among friends and relatives)

Āp
आप

(polite; among strangers and acquaintances, but regionally also among friends and relatives)

He/She	Vah वह
We	Ham हम

(colloquial: **ham-log** = "we folks")

You (plural)	Tum तुम

(among friends and relatives; to differentiate between this **tum** and the singular form **tum**, colloquially the form **tum-log** = "you folks" may be used)

Āp
आप

(to differentiate between the singular **āp**, one could informally say **āp-log** = "you folks")

They (over here) Ye
ये

They (over there) Ve
वे

Don't! Nā karnā!
ना करना !

Please! Kripayā!/Kripā karke!
कृपया !/कृपा करके !

Thank you. Dhanyavād/Shukriyā.
धन्यवाद/शुक्रिया ।

You're welcome! Koī bāt nahīñ!
कोई बात नहीं !

Literally, the Hindi sentence simply means "It's no matter." On the other hand, "Welcome!" in the sense of welcoming a guest is **svāgat!** In very formal circumstances, sometimes the Sanskrit word **svāgatam!** is used.

Don't mention it!	Koī bāt nahīñ! कोई बात नहीं !
That's all right.	Ṭhīk hai. ठीक है ।
Could you...?	Mumkin ho ki āp...? मुमकिन हो कि आप ... ?
Do you know...?	Āp jānte haiñ ki ...? आप जानते हैं कि ... ?
Do you have...?	Āp ke pās ... hai? आप के पास ... है ?
I'd like...	Mujhe .... cāhi(y)e. मुझे ... चाहिए ।
Shall I/Can I/May I ... ?	Maiñ ...-ūñ? मैं ... -ऊं ?

Note: This cannot be translated literally without verb. A Hindi speaker would use the subjunctive form of a verb, which is formed by adding **-ūñ** to its stem; the stem being the verb minus the ending **-nā**.

Example: **karnā** = to do: The stem is **kar-**, to which one would add **-ūñ** and get **karūñ. Maiñ karūñ?** = Shall/Can/May I do? Or, with **jānā** = to go: The stem of **jānā** is **jā-**; add **-ūñ** to get **jāūñ. Maiñ jāūñ?** = Shall/Can/May I go?

Can I have that?	Yah mil saktā hai, kyā? यह मिल सकता है, क्या ?
How much is this?	Yah kaise diyā jātā hai? यह कैसे दिया जाता है ?

Literally, "How is this given?" Alternatively, you could say **Yah kitne kā hai?** = "Of how much is this?"

That's so cheap. Yah bahut sastā hai.
यह बहुत सस्ता है ।

Note to bargain hunters: Never say this to a salesman, unless you want to witness instant inflation!

That's expensive. Yah mahaṅgā hai.
यह महँगा है ।

I'm not buying that. Yah maiñ nahīñ kharīdūñgā ♂/ kharidūñgī ♀.
यह मैं नहीं ख़रीदूँगा/ख़रीदूँगी ।

Make it cheaper and I'll buy it. Dām thoṛā kam kīji(y)e, to kharīdūñgā ♂/ kharīdūñgī ♀.
दाम थोड़ा कम कीजिए, तो ख़रीदूँगा/ख़रीदूँगी ।

This price is OK. Yahīñ dām sahī hai.
यहीं दाम सही है ।

Can you do it?	Tum yah kar sakoge ♂/sakogī ♀? तुम यह कर सकोगे/सकोगी ?
I can do it.	Maiñ yah kar saktā ♂/saktī ♀ hūñ. मैं यह कर सकता/सकती हूँ ।
I can't do it.	Maiñ yah nahīñ kar saktā ♂/saktī ♀. मैं यह नहीं कर सकता/सकती ।
I'll do it.	Maiñ yah karūñgā ♂/karūñgī ♀. मैं यह करूँगा/करूँगी ।
I've got to do it.	Mujhe yah karnā paṛegā. मुझे यह करना पड़ेगा ।

Got a Minute? 3

One moment, please.	Kripā karke, ek miniṭ. कृपा करके, एक मिनिट।
When?	Kab? कब ?
Till when?	Kab tak? कब तक ?
About when?	Lagbhag/Taḵrīban kab? लगभग/तक़रीबन कब ?
What time?	Kitne baje? कितने बजे ?

Is that too early?	Yah kāfī jaldī hai? यह काफ़ी जल्दी है ?
Is that too late?	Yah der hī hai? यह देर ही है ?

What time is it convenient for you?	Āp ke li(y)e kitne baje lāyak hai? आप के लिए कितने बजे लायक़ है ?
What day is it convenient for you?	Āp ke li(y)e kaunsā din lāyak hai? आप के लिए कौनसा दिन लायक़ है ?
How about tomorrow?	Kal calegā? कल चलेगा ?
How about the day after tomorrow?	Parsoñ calegā? परसों चलेगा ?
Today is better.	Āj behtar hī hai. आज बेहतर ही है ।
Yesterday/ Tomorrow.	Kal. कल ।
The day before yesterday/ The day after tomorrow.	Parsoñ. परसों ।

Note: Oddly, Hindi uses the same word for "yesterday" and "tomorrow", and respectively, the same word for "the day before yesterday" and "the day after tomorrow". Only in the context of a sentence can one determine if **kal** or **parsoñ** are addressed to past or future. One could speculate that ancient Indians lived strictly in the "here and now" and past or future didn't even warrant a separate vocabulary. Neat.

What (week)day is today?	Āj kaunsā din/vār hai? आज कौनसा दिन/वार है ?
Today's Monday.	Āj somvār hai. आज सोमवार है ।
Tuesday.	Maṅgalvār. मंगलवार ।

Wednesday.	Budhvār. बुधवार।
Thursday.	Guruvār/Brihaspativār. गुरुवार/बृहस्पतिवार।

Note: Both **guruvār** and **brihaspativār** are used with regional differences. In Punjab und Haryana the word **vīrvār** is also heard.

Friday.	Shukravār/Jumā (Jumā is used among Muslims). शुक्रवार/जुमा।
Saturday.	Shanivār. शनिवार।
Sunday.	Ravivār/Itvār. रविवार/इतवार।
How about the 18th?	Aṭhārahvīñ tārīkh ṭhīk hai? अठारहवीं तारीख़ ठीक है ?

Note: Aṭhārahvīñ tārīkh, literally "18th date".

The 1st ... (of a month)	pahlī tārīkh पहली तारीख़

Note: **tārīkh** = date

The 2nd ...	dūsrī tārīkh दूसरी तारीख़
The 3rd ...	tīsrī tārīkh तीसरी तारीख़
The 4th ...	cauthī tārīkh चौथी तारीख़
The 5th ...	pāñcvīñ tārīkh पाँचवीं तारीख़
The 6th ...	chaṭhī tārīkh छठी तारीख़

The 7th ...	sātvīñ tārīkh सातवीं तारीख़
The 8th ...	āṭhvīñ tārīkh आठवीं तारीख़
The 9th ...	navīñ tārīkh नवीं तारीख़
The 10th ...	dasvīñ tārīkh दसवीं तारीख़
The 11th ...	gyārahvīñ tārīkh ग्यारहवीं तारीख़
The 12th ...	bārahvīñ tārīkh बारहवीं तारीख़
The 13th ...	terahvīñ tārīkh तेरहवीं तारीख़
The 14th ...	caudahvīñ tārīkh चौदहवीं तारीख़
The 15th ...	pandrahvīñ tārīkh पंद्रहवीं तारीख़
The 16th ...	solahvīñ tārīkh सोलहवीं तारीख़
The 17th ...	satrahvīñ tārīkh सत्रहवीं तारीख़
The 18th ...	aṭhārahvīñ tārīkh अठारहवीं तारीख़
The 19th ...	unnīsvīñ tārīkh उन्नीसवीं तारीख़
The 20th ...	bīsvīñ tārīkh बीसवीं तारीख़

The 21st …	ikkīsvīñ tārī<u>kh</u> इक्कीसवीं तारीख़
The 22nd …	bāīsvīñ tārī<u>kh</u> बाईसवीं तारीख़
The 23rd …	teīsvīñ tārī<u>kh</u> तेईसवीं तारीख़
The 24th …	caubīsvīñ tārī<u>kh</u> चौबीसवीं तारीख़
The 25th …	paccīsvīñ tārī<u>kh</u> पच्चीसवीं तारीख़
The 26th …	cabbīsvīñ tārī<u>kh</u> चब्बीसवीं तारीख़
The 27th …	sattāīsvīñ tārī<u>kh</u> सत्ताईसवीं तारीख़
The 28th …	aṭṭhāīsvīñ tārī<u>kh</u> अट्ठाईसवीं तारीख़
The 29th …	untīsvīñ tārī<u>kh</u> उनतीसवीं तारीख़
The 30th …	tīsvīñ tārī<u>kh</u> तीसवीं तारीख़
The 31st …	ikatīsvīñ tārī<u>kh</u> इकतीसवीं तारीख़
January	janvarī जनवरी
February	farvarī फ़रवरी
March	mārc मार्च

April	aprail अप्रैल
May	maī मई
June	jūn जून
July	julāī जुलाई
August	agast अगस्त
September	si(p)tambar सितंबर
October	aktūbar अक्तूबर
November	navambar नवंबर
December	disambar दिसंबर
On January 1.	Pahlī janvarī ko. पहली जनवरी को।
On January 2.	Dūsrī janvarī ko. दूसरी जनवरी को।
On March 3.	Tīsrī mārc ko. तीसरी मार्च को।
On April 4.	Chauthī aprail ko. छौथी अप्रैल को।
On May 5. (and so forth)	Pāñcvīñ maī ko. पाँचवीं मई को।

Could it be sooner?	Is ke jaldī ho saktā hai? इस के जल्दी हो सकता है ?
I'd rather make it later.	Der hī behtar hogā. देर ही बेहतर होगा ।
One/Two/Three/Four/Five o'clock.	Ek/do/tīn/cār/pāñc baje. एक/दो/तीन/चार/पाँच बजे ।
Half past one.	Ḍeṛh baje. डेढ़ बजे ।
Half past two.	Ḍhāī baje. ढाई बजे ।
Half past three.	Sāṛhe tīn baje. साढ़े तीन बजे ।
Half past four.	Sāṛhe cār baje. साढ़े चार बजे ।
Half past five.	Sāṛhe pāñc baje. साढ़े पाँच बजे ।
Half past six.	Sāṛhe chah baje. साढ़े छ: बजे ।

Etc.

Note: To express "half past", in most cases the word **sāṛhe** is used, which loosely translates as "plus a half". It is placed in front of the numeral which is to have half added to its value. So: **sāṛhe tīn** = a half plus three = 3 ½. Exceptions are 1 ½ and 2 ½, for which Hindi has special words: **ḍeṛh** = 1 ½, **ḍhāī** = 2 ½.

In the morning.	Subah ko. सुबह को ।
Early in the morning.	Subah-savere. सुबह-सवेरे ।

In the afternoon.	Dopahar ko. दोपहर को।
In the evening.	Shām ko. शाम को।
At night.	Rāt ko. रात को।

Note: There is no particular word for midday, one would simply say **bārah baje ko** = at 12 o'clock.

Midnight.	Ādhī rāt. आधी रात।

Literally "Half the night"

Too early.	Kāfī jaldī. काफ़ी जल्दी।
Too late.	Kāfī der. काफ़ी देर।
On time.	Ṭhīk samay par. ठीक समय पर।

Then when can you make it?	Kitne baje ā sakoge ♂/sakogī ♀? कितने बजे आ सकोगे/सकोगी ?
What time can I come over?	Kitne baje ā sakūñgā ♂/ sakūñgī ♀? कितने बजे सकूँगा/सकूँगी ?
What time do we leave?	Ham kitne baje cale jā(y)eñge ♂/ calī jā(y)eñgī ♀? हम कितने बजे चले जाएँगे/ चली जाएँगी ?
What time do we arrive?	Ham kitne baje pahuñceñge ♂/ pahuñceñgī ♀? हम कितने बजे पहुंचेंगे/पहुंचेंगी ?
What time will you be back?	Tum kitne baje vāpas āoge ♂/ āogī ♀? तुम कितने बजे वापस आओगे/ आओगी ?
Are you ready?	Taiyār ho? तैयार हो ?
When will you do it?	Tum vah kab karoge ♂/karogī ♀? तुम वह कब करोगे / करोगी ?
When will it be finished?	Kām kab pūrā hogā? काम कब पूरा होगा ?
How long will it take?	Kitnā ṭāim lagegā? कितना टाइम लगेगा ?
I'll be done soon.	Kām jaldī ho jā(y)egā. काम जल्दी हो जाएगा ।
Not now.	Abhī nahīñ. अभी नहीं ।

Maybe later.	Shāyad bād meñ. शायद बाद में ।
Not yet.	Ab tak nahīñ. अब तक नहीं ।
Next time.	Āgli dafā/bār. आगली दफ़ा/बार ।
Previously.	Pahle. पहले ।
I don't know when.	Mujhe patā/mālūm nahīñ kab. मुझे पता/मालूम नहीं कब ।
I don't know yet.	Mujhe ab tak patā/mālūm nahīñ. मुझे अब तक पता/मालूम नहीं ।
Sometime.	Kabhī na kabhī. कभी न कभी ।
Someday.	Koī ānevāle din. कोई आनेवाले दिन ।
Always.	Hameshā. हमेशा ।
Every day.	(Har) Roz. (हर) रोज़ ।
Never again!	Phir kabhī nahīñ! फिर कभी नहीं !
Don't do that ever again!	Aisā āindā mat karnā! ऐसा आइंदा मत करना !
Any time is fine.	Kabhī bhī ṭhīk hai. कभी भी ठीक है ।

You decide when.	Tumhāri marzī. तुम्हारी मरज़ी।

Note: Tumhāri marzī can also be translated as "Whenever you like", literally it means "As you please."

That day is fine.	Us din ṭhīk hai. उस दिन ठीक है।
Okay, let's meet then.	To ṭhīk hai, mileñ. तो ठीक है, मिलें।
That's not a good day for me.	Vah din mere li(y)e lāyak nahīñ. वह दिन मेरे लिए लायक़ नहीं।
Let's begin.	Shurū kareñ. शुरू करें।
Let's continue.	Āge kareñ. आगे करें।
Let's start again.	Phir se shurū kareñ. फिर मे शुरू करें।
Let's do it later.	Vah bād meñ kareñ. वह बाद में करें।
Do it later!	Vah bād meñ karo! वह बाद में करो!
It'll only take a minute.	Sirf ek hī miniṭ lagegā. सिर्फ़ एक ही मिनिट लगेगा।
Hurry up!	Jaldī karo! जल्दी करो !
I'll do it quickly.	Maiñ vah jaldī karūñgā♂/ karūñgī♀. मैं वह जल्दी करूँगा/करूँगी

I'll finish soon.	Maiñ vah jaldī pūrā karūñgā ♂/ karūñgī ♀. मैं वह जल्दी पूरा करूँगा/करूंगी।
I've finished.	Maiñ ne kām pūrā kiyā. मैं ने काम पूरा किया।
Have you finished?	Tum ne kām pūrā kiyā? तुम ने काम पूरा किया ?

Say What! 4

Listen! Sunnā!/Sun!/Suno!/Suni(y)e!/ Suni(y)egā!
सुनना !/सुन !/सुनो !/सुनिए !/ सुनिएगा !

Whereas there is only one imperative in English, there are five different imperatives in Hindi. The five forms convey different levels of politeness. **Sunnā** is simply the infinitive of the verb "to listen" and it can also be used as a somewhat crude imperative. Similarly, **sun**—the root of the infinitive—carries a rough undertone. Both can be used among good friends or close relatives. **Suno** is slightly more polite and can be used among acquaintances or in casual everyday speech; but don't use it in front of persons of authority or high standing. **Suni(y)e** is the polite word of choice; one could translate it as "please listen". **Suni(y)egā** is extra-polite ("Would you kindly listen?") and rarely heard in everyday encounters.

Listen to what I'm saying! Merī bāt suno!
मेरी बात सुनो !

Don't ask me that!	Mujh se yah mat pūchnā! मुझ से यह मत पूछना !
Can you hear me?	Mujhe sun sakte ♂/saktī ♀ ho? मुझे सुन सकते/सकती हो ?
Did you hear me?	Mujhe sunā ♂/sunī ♀? मुझे सुना/सुनी ?
I couldn't hear.	Maiñ sun nahīñ sakā ♂/sakī ♀. मैं सुन नहीं सका/सकी ।
I don't want to hear about that.	Us ke bāre meñ mujhe nahīñ sunnā cāhi(y)e. उस के बारे मैं मुझे नहीं सुनना चाहिए ।
Could I ask you for something?	Āp se koī bintī karūñ? आप से कोई बिनती करूँ ?
What are you talking about?	Āp kis ke bāre meñ bāt kar rahe ♂/rahī ♀ haiñ? आप किस के बारे में बात कर रहे/रही हैं ?
You shouldn't say such things.	Aisī cīzeñ nahīñ bolnā hai. ऐसी चीज़ें नहीं बोलना है ।

Note: Or, very colloquially: **Aisī cīzeñ na bolne kā.**

I didn't say anything.	Maiñ kuch nahīñ bolā ♂/bolī ♀. मैं कुछ नहीं बोला/बोली ।
Let's talk in Hindi.	Hindī meñ bāt kareñ. हिंदी में बात करें ।
Can you speak Hindi?	Āp hindī bol sakte ♂/saktī ♀ haiñ? आप हिंदी बोल सकते/सकती हैं ?

I don't speak any Hindi.	Maiñ hindī nahīñ bol saktā♂/ saktī♀. मैं हिंदी नहीं बोल सकता/सकती ।
I speak a little Hindi.	Maiñ thoṛī-sī hindī bol saktā♂/ saktī♀. मैं थोड़ी-सी हिंदी बोल सकता/ सकती ।
Do you speak English?	Āp aṅgrezī bol sakte♂/ saktī♀ haiñ? आप अंग्रेज़ी बोल सकते/सकती हैं ?
Is there anyone who speaks English?	Yahāñ koī aṅgrezī bolne-vālā hai? यहाँ कोई अंग्रेज़ी बोलने-वाला है ?
Let's talk about it later.	Us ke bāre meñ bād meñ bāt kareñ. उस के बारे में बाद में बात करें ।
Tell me later.	Mujhe bād meñ batāo! मुझे बाद में बताओ !
I don't feel like talking.	Bāt karne kā man nahīñ lagtā. बात करने का मन नहीं लगता ।

Note: "To be in the mood for this" or to "feel like this" is **man lagnā**, which roughly translates as "having a mind to …". Further examples of usage: **khāne kā man nahīñ lagtā** = I don't feel like eating; **jāne kā man nahīñ lagtā** = I don't feel like going; **ghar jāne kā man nahīñ lagtā** = I don't feel like going home. Of course, by dropping the **nahīñ** (not), the sentences will get a positive meaning.

Don't ask me that.	Yah mujh se mat pūcho. यह मुझ से मत पूछो ।

Note: This is a neutral alternative to the more emphatic **Muji se yah mat pūchnā!**

I don't want to talk about it.	Maiñ us ke bāre meñ bāt nahīñ karnā cāhtā♂/cāhtī♀. मैं उस के बारे में बात नहीं करना चाहता/चाहती ।
Don't make excuses.	Bahānā mat banāo! बहाना मत बनाओ !
That's not a good excuse.	Yah koī bahānā nahīñ. यह कोई बहाना नहीं ।
Stop complaining!	Shikāyateñ mat kiyā karo! शिकायतें मत किया करो !
Don't talk so loud.	Itnī ūñcī āvāz se mat bol! इतनी ऊंची आवाज़ से मत बोल !
Speak up!	Zor se bol! ज़ोर से बोल !
Speak more slowly, please!	Kripayā, āhistā boli(y)e! कृपया, आहिस्ता बोलिए !
Say it again!	Dubārā bol! दुबारा बोल !
I beg your pardon?	Punah kahi(y)e. पुनः कहिए ।

What did you say?	Āp ne kyā kahā? आप ने क्या कहा ?
What?	Kyā? क्या ?
Do you understand?	Āp samajh rahe ♂/rahī ♀ haiñ? आप समझ रहे/रही हैं ?
I understand.	Maiñ samajh rahā ♂/rahī ♀ hūñ. मैं समझ रहा/रही हुँ।
I don't understand.	Maiñ nahīñ samajh rahā ♂/rahī ♀. मैं नहीं समझ रहा/रही हुँ।
What does that mean?	Is kā matlab kyā hai? इस का मतलब क्या है ?
Did you say that?	Kyā āp ne yah kahā? क्या आप मे यह कहा ?
I didn't say that.	Maiñ ne yah nahīñ kahā. मैं ने यह नहीं कहा।
I didn't say anything.	Maiñ ne kuch nahīñ kahā. मैं ने कुछ नहीं कहा।
I didn't tell anyone.	Maiñ ne kisī ko nahīñ batāyā. मैं ने किसी को नहीं बताया।
I won't tell anyone.	Maiñ kisī ko batāūñgā ♂/ batāūñgī ♀ nahīñ. मैं किसी को बताऊँगा/बताऊँगी नहीं।
Say hello to … for me.	… ko mere praṇām dīji(y)e. … को मेरे प्रणाम दीजिए।

Literally "Give my regards/greetings to ..", quite a polite way of talking and endearing yourself.

Look at That! 5

Look!	Dekho! देखो !
Look at this!	Yah dekho! यह देखो !
Look at that!	Vah dekho! वह देखो !
Take a look.	Zarā-sā dekho. ज़रा-सा देखो !
Don't look!	Dekho mat! देखो मत !
Can you see it?	Yah dekh sakte ♂/saktī ♀ ho? यह देख सकते/सकती हो ?
Did you see it?	Tum ne yah dekhā? तुम ने यह देखा ?
I saw it.	Maiñ ne yah dekhā. मैं ने यह देखा ।
I didn't see it.	Maiñ ne yah nahīñ dekhā. मैं ने यह नहीं देखा ।
I don't want to see it.	Maiñ yah dekhnā nahīñ cāhtā ♂/cāhtī ♀. मैं यह देखना नहीं चाहता/चाहती ।

I want to see you soon.	Maiñ tum se turant milnā cāhtā♂/cāhtī♀ hūñ. मैं तुम से तुरंत मिलना चाहता/चाहती हूँ ।
I've been wanting to see you.	Bahut ṭāim se tum se milnā cāhtā♂/cāhtī♀ thā. बहुत टाइम से तुम से मिलना चाहता/चाहती था ।
I saw Paul the other day.	Kaī din pahle maiñ ne Paul ko dekhā. कई दिन पहले मैं ने पौल को देखा ।
I'm going to see (meet) Paul next week.	Āgle hafte maiñ Paul se milūñgā♂/milūñgī♀. आगले हफ़्ते मैं पौल से मिलूँगा/मिलूँगी ।
So let's meet again!	To phir se mileñ! तो फिर से मिलें !
See you later.	Bād meñ mileñge♂/mileñgī♀. बाद में मिलेंगे/मिलेंगी ।

See you soon.	Jaldī mileñge ♂/mileñgī ♀. जल्दी मिलेंगे/मिलेंगी ।
I'll show you.	Maiñ tum ko dikhāūñgā ♂/ dikhāūñgī ♀. मैं तुम को दिखाऊँगा/दिखाऊँगी ।

Coming & Going 6

Come here!	Idhar āo! इधर आओ !
Visit me.	Mere ghar [meñ] āo. मेरे घर [में] आओ ।
I'll come over soon.	Maiñ turant āūñgā ♂/āūñgī ♀. मैं तुरंत आऊँगा/आऊँगी ।
Come later.	Bād meñ āo. बाद में आओ ।
Can you come?	Ā sakte ♂/saktī ♀ ho? आ सकते/सकती हो ?
Come along with us.	Hamāre sāth āo. हमारे साथ आओ ।
Could you come with me, please?	Yahāñ ā(y)egā ♂/ ā(y)egī ♀ ? यहाँ आएगा / आएगी ?
He's/She's coming here.	Vah yahāñ ā rahā ♂/rahī ♀ hai. वह यहाँ आ रहा/रही है ।
I'll be right here!	Āyā ♂/āyī ♀! आया/आयी !

Literally, "I came", implying that it won't take long until he/she has come—well, he/she's virtually come already.

I'll go soon.	Maiñ turant jāūñgā ♂/jāūñgī ♀. मैं तुरंत जाऊँगा/जाऊँगी ।

I can go.	Maiñ jā saktā♂/saktī♀ hūñ. मैं जा सकता/सकती हूँ।
I think I can go.	Mere khayāl se maiñ jā sakūñgā♂/sakūñgī♀. मेरे ख़याल से मैं जा सकूँगा/सकूँगी।
I can't go.	Maiñ jā nahīñ saktā♂/saktī♀. मैं जा नहीं सकता/सकती।
I want to go.	Maiñ jānā cāhtā♂/cāhtī♀ hūñ. मैं जाना चाहता/चाहती हूँ।
I want to go to Delhi/Mumbai/Kolkata.	Maiñ Dillī/Mumbaī/Kolkātā jānā cāhtā♂/cāhtī♀ hūñ. मैं दिल्ली/मुंबई/कोलकाता जाना चाहता/चाहती हूँ।
I really want to go.	Mujhe bilkul jānā cāhi(y)e. मुझे बिलकुल जाना चाहिए।
I don't want to go.	Muhje jāne kā man nahīñ lagtā. मुझे जाने का मन नहीं लगता।
You're going, aren't you?	Jāoge♂/Jāogī♀, na? जाओगे/जाओगी, न ?
You went, didn't you?	Gayā♂/Gayī♀ ki nahīñ? गया/गयी कि नहीं ?
I'm going.	Maiñ jā rahā♂/rahī♀ hūñ. मैं जा रहा/रही हूँ।
I'm not going.	Maiñ nahīñ jā rahā♂/rahī♀ hūñ. मैं नहीं जा रहा/रही हूँ।
I went.	Maiñ gayā♂/gayī♀. मैं गया/गयी।
I didn't go.	Maiñ nahīñ gayā♂/gayī♀. मैं नहीं गया/गयी।

Don't go!	Jāo mat! जाओ मत !
Don't go yet.	Abhī mat jāo! अभी मत जाओ !
I have to go.	Mujhe jānā hai. मुझे जाना है ।
I must go now.	Mujhe abhī jānā hai. मुझे अभी जाना है ।
May I go?	Maiñ jāuñ? मैं जाऊँ ?
Shall we go?	Ham jāeñ? हम जाएँ ?
Let's go.	Caleñ. चलें ।
Let's leave here.	Yahāñ se caleñ. यहाँ से चलें ।
I'm going to leave.	Maiñ calā jāūñgā ♂/calī jāūñgī ♀. मैं चला जाऊँगा/चली जाऊँगी ।
When are you leaving?	Kab caloge ♂/calogī ♀? कब चलोगे/चलोगी ?
I'm leaving tomorrow.	Maiñ kal calā jāūñgā ♂/ calī jāūñgī ♀. मैं कल चला जाऊँगा/चली जाऊँगी ।
I'm leaving soon.	Maiñ jaldī calā jāūñgā ♂/ calī jāūñgī ♀. मैं जल्दी चला जाऊँगा/ चली जाऊँगी ।

He/She has left here. Vah yahāñ se calā gayā ♂/ calī gayī ♀.
वह यहाँ से चला गया/चली गयी।

Stay here. Yahāñ pe rahnā.
यहाँ पे रहना।

Where are you going? Tum kahāñ jā rahe ♂ /rahī ♀ ho?
तुम कहाँ जा रहे/रही हो ?

Please go first!/ After you! Pahle tum!
पहले तुम।

Actually, the Hindi sentence simply means "You first" and can be applied in a variety of situations. A more polite variant is **pahle āp.** It's the base of a very common joke, in which one polite person says to the other "after you, please", and the other responds "no, after *you*", and both of them keep insisting and no one ever goes.

Go slowly! Āhistā jāo!
आहिस्ता जाओ !

Go straight ahead. Sīdhā jāo!
सीधा जाओ !

BUS & TRAIN

Which bus/train should one take to get to ...?	.... jāne ke li(y)e kaunsī bas/ṭren pakaṛnā hai? ...जाने के लिए कौनसी बस/ ट्रेन पकड़ना है ?
Which station does one have to get off to go to ...?	... jāne ke li(y)e kis sṭeshan pe utarnā paṛegā? ...जाने के लिए किस स्टेशन पे उतरना पड़ेगा ?
Does this bus/train go to ...?	Yah bas/ṭren ... jātī hai? यह बस/ट्रेन ... जाती है ?
Where do I get the ticket?	Ṭikaṭ kahāñ milegā? टिकट कहाँ मिलेगा ?
Where is the bus stop/train station?	Bas stop/ṭren sṭeshan kahāñ hai? बस स्टाप/ट्रेन स्टेशन कहाँ है ?

Eat, Drink & Be Merry! 7

I'm hungry.	Mujhe bhūkh lagī. मुझे भूख लगी।
I'm starving.	Mujhe bahut bhūkh lagī. मुझे बहुत भूख लगी।
I'd like to eat something.	Mujhe kuch khānā cāhi(y)e. मुझे कुछ खाना चाहिए।
Have you eaten?	Tum ne khānā khāyā? तुम ने खाना खाया ?

Note: Or just short **khānā khāya**? It's probably the most frequently asked question in India. Sometimes it's almost used as a greeting. It's supposed to signal concern for the other person.

I haven't eaten yet.	Maiñ ne khānā nahīñ khāyā. मैं ने खाना नहीं खाया ।
Do you want to eat something?	Kuch khānā cāhi(y)e? कुछ खाना चाहिए ?
I don't want to eat.	Mujhe khānā nahīñ cāhi(y)e. मुझे खाना नहीं चाहिए ।
I won't eat.	Mujh se khānā nahīñ hogā. मुझ से खाना नहीं होगा ।
Do you want to eat some more?	Aur kuch khānā cāhi(y)e? और कुछ खाना चाहिए ?
What would you like to eat?	Tum ko kyā khānā cāhi(y)e? तुम को क्या खाना चाहिए ?
I'm thirsty.	Mujhe pyās lagī. मुझे प्यास लगी ।
Do you want to drink something?	Tum ko kuch pīnā cāhi(y)e? तुम को कुछ पीना चाहिए ?
I'd like to drink beer.	Mujhe bīr pīnā cāhi(y)e. मुझे बीर पीना चाहिए ।
This tastes kind of weird.	Is kā svād ajīb–sā hai. इस का स्वाद अजीब-सा है ।
I think this has gone bad.	Mere khayāl se vah kharāb ho gayā hai. मेरे ख़याल से वह ख़राब हो गया है ।
I want some liquor.	Mujhe sharāb cāhi(y)e. मुझे शराब चाहिए ।
What kind of liquor is that?	Yah kaisī sharāb hai? यह कैसी शराब है ?

This is home-brewed liquor.	Yah deshī sharāb hai. यह देशी शराब है।

Note: Cheap liquor, often illegally produced, is widely available in small "bars"—well, shacks (colloquially called **aḍḍā**) might often be a better description. Depending on its main ingredient, the liquor may be called **santrā, nārāṅgi** (both made from fermented oranges) or **ṭharrā** (from the fruit of the mahua tree).

I don't want to drink.	Mujhe pīnā nahīñ cāhi(y)e. मुझे पीना नहीं चाहिए।
I won't drink.	Mujh se pīnā nahīñ hogā. मुझ से पीना नहीं होगा।
I haven't drunk yet.	Maiñ ne kuch piyā nahīñ. मैं ने कुछ पिया नहीं।
Do you want to drink some more?	Tum ko aur kuch pīnā cāhi(y)e? तुम को और कुछ पीना चाहिए ?
Thank you, but I still have some.	Nahīñ jī, kuch bāḵī hai. नहीं जी, कुछ बाक़ी है।
Come on, drink a little bit more.	Are, aur kuch piyā karo! अरे, और कुछ पिया करो !
It's on me.	Merī round hai. मेरी राउंड है।
The next round's on me.	Aglī round mere♂/merī♀ ūpar hai. अगली राउंड मेरे/मेरी ऊपर है।
Cheers!	Cheers ! चीर्स !

There is no real word for it in Hindi, as traditional Indian culture does not encourage drinking alcohol. In Hindi movies, if a character drinks alcohol it's usually an indication that he or she is a bad character.

How about some dinner?	Kyā, shām kā bhojan lene kā? क्या, शाम का भोजन लेने का ?
Have you ordered?	Order diyā ki nahīñ? आर्दर दिया कि नहीं ?
Is that food vegetarian?	Yah khānā veg/shākāhārī hai? यह खाना वेज/शाकाहारी है ?
No, that food isn't vegetarian/ contains meat.	Nahīñ, yah khānā non–veg/ māṃsāhārī hai. नहीं, यह खाना नॉन-वेज/ मांसाहारी है ।

Note: In India, vegetarian food isn't by any means exotic: About 30% of the population are vegetarians, mostly Hindus and Jains. Virtually all restaurants cater to vegetarians, if they're not completely vegetarian in the first place. Often, the English short forms veg/non-veg are used, but if you want to impress your hosts, employ the more bookish terms **shākāhārī** (= vegetable-eating) and **maṃsāhārī** (= meat-eating).

Is the meal ready?	Khānā taiyār hai? खाना तैयार है ?
It's ready.	Taiyār hai. तैयार है ।
Enjoy your meal!	Mauj se khāo! मौज से खाओ !
Eat your fill!	<u>Kh</u>ūb khāo! खूब खाओ !
That looks delicious.	Vah mazedār lag rahā hai. वह मज़ेदार लग रहा है ।
Please bring three plates of this!	Is kā tīn jagaheñ dījiye! इस का तीन जगहें दीजिए !

Note: "A plate" here literally translates as "place" (**jagah**).

This is a feast!	Kyā dāvat hai! क्या दावत है !
Wow, this tastes good!	Vāh, kyā svād hai! वाह, क्या स्वाद है !
Yum! Yum!	Vāh–vāh, kyā khānā! वाह-वाह, क्या खाना !

Literally "Wow, what food!"

The food tastes like shit.	Khānā ekdam bakvās hai. खाना एकदम बकवास है !

Note: Indians don't share the Western fixation with faecal matter, and they and don't use the word "shit" in curses—unless they are very Westernised; but in that case they'd more likely converse in English anyway. The above Hindi sentence literally means "The food is totally nonsense." You can use the ... **bakvās hai** in many other instances, for example **Yah movie bakvās hai.** = This movie is crap. Add **ekdam** to **bakvās** and it becomes "totally crap".

Do you want more food?	Tum ko aur kuch khānā cāhi(y)e? तुम को और कुछ खाना चाहिए ?
I'd like more food.	Mujhe aur kuch khānā cāhi(y)e. मुझे और कुछ खाना चाहिए ।
Give me a little more.	Mujhe thoṛā–sā aur do. मुझे थोड़ा-सा और दो ।
Enough?	Bas? बस ?
Enough.	Bas ho gayā. बस हो गया ।
Not enough (I want more).	Aur cāhi(y)e. और चाहिए ।

What's this?	Yah kyā hai? यह क्या है ?
Taste it.	Svād lo. स्वाद लो ।
I can't eat that.	Yah maiñ nahīñ khā saktā ♂/ saktī ♀. यह मैं नहीं खा सकता/सकती ।
What's that stuff?	Yah kyā cīz hai? यह क्या चीज़ है ?
Is it spicy?	Tīkhā hai? तीखा है ?
Yuck!	Chī!/Chī-chī! छी !/छी-छी !

Note: You can use **chī/chī-chī** for anything disgusting, shameful or unsavory, like the old English "fie". More examples: **Chī-chī, yahāñ peshāb nahīñ karne kā!** = "Disgusting, you shouldn't piss here!"

Chī-chī, kyā besharam bāteñ! "How disgusting this shameless talk!" **Chī-chī, yah jagah kitnī gandī hai!** = "Disgusting how dirty this place is!"

It doesn't taste good.	Us kā svād ṭhīk nahīñ. उस का स्वाद ठीक नहीं ।
It's awful.	Vah ekdam bekār hai. वह एकदम बेकार है ।
Water, water!	Pānī, pānī! पानी, पानी !

My mouth's on fire!	Merī mūñh meñ āg lag gayī hai. मेरी मूंह में आग लग गयी है।
How do you eat this?	Yah kaise khāyā jātā hai? यह कैसे खाया जाता है ?
Please bring me a fork/knife/spoon!	Mujhe ek kāṇṭā/cāḵū/cammac dījiye! मुझे एक कांटा/चाक़ू/चम्मच दीजिए !

Note: A derivation of **cammac** (spoon) is **camcā**. Taken literally, a **camcā** is someone who spoon-feeds you flattery and grovels up to you, especially if you're in a position of power or influence. One can translate it as "sycophant" or "flatterer". Usually, Indian politicians are surrounded by a coterie of **camce** (plural of **camcā**).

Do you want a fork/knife/spoon?	Tum ko ek kāṇṭā/cāḵū/cammac cāhi(y)e? तुम को एक कांटा/चाक़ू/चम्मच चाहिए ?

Could you pack the remainder in a bag, please! Bākī jo rahā, parcel banāke dījiye!
बाक़ी जो रहा, पार्सल बनाके दीजिए !

When Hindi speakers ask for a take-away, they say—depending on grade of politeness—**parcel banāke denā/de/d(e)o/dīji(y)e/dīji(y)egā!** = Make it into a parcel! Note the five available imperatives as mentioned before (page 51). Surprisingly, even hot tea is often poured into a plastic bag as take-away.

Now it's my turn to stand a meal! Ab merī barī khānā khilāne kī!
अब मेरी बरी खाना खिलाने की !

Getting Emotional 8

I like this.	Yah mujhe pasand hai. यह मुझे पसंद है ।
Which do you like best?	In meñ tum ko kaunsā acchā lagtā hai? इन में तुम को कौनसा अच्छा लगता है ?
I like it a lot.	Mujhe bahut pasand hai. मुझे बहुत पसंद है ।
I enjoyed it very much.	Yah mujhe bahut acchā lagā. यह मुझे बहुत अच्छा लगा ।
I don't like it.	Yah mujhe pasand nahīñ. यह मुझे पसंद नहीं ।
I hate it.	Maiñ us ko nafrat kartā♂/kartī♀ hūñ. मैं उस को नफ़रत करता/करती हूँ ।
I can't stand it.	Yah mujh se bardāsht nahīñ hotā. यह मुझ से बरदाश्त नहीं होता ।
No, thank you.	Jī nahīñ. जी नहीं ।
I want... (+ verb).	Maiñ ... cāhtā♂/cāhtī♀ hūñ. मैं ... चाहता/चाहती हूँ ।

I want ... (+ noun). Mujhe ... cāhi(y)e.
मुझे ... चाहिए।

I don't want ... Mujhe ... nahīñ cāhi(y)e.
मुझे ... नहीं चाहिए।

I don't need this. Is kī mujhe koī zarūrat nahīñ.
इस की मुझे कोई ज़रूरत नहीं।

This is no good. Yah acchā nahīñ.
यह अच्छा नहीं।

This is not what I expected. Maiñ ne yahī ummīd nahīñ kī.
मैं ने यही उम्मीद नहीं की।

I'm busy. Maiñ busy hūñ.
मैं बिज़ी हूँ।

There is a proper Hindi word for "busy" (**vyast**), but it's hardly used in a modern context and would sound a bit odd.

I'm happy. Maiñ <u>kh</u>ush hūñ.
मैं खुश हूँ।

I'm pleased to hear that. Yah sunkar mujhe bahut <u>kh</u>ushī huī.
यह सुनकर मुझे बहुत खुशी हुई।

I'm sad. Maiñ udās hūñ.
मैं उदास हूँ।

I'm fine. Maiñ ṭhīk hūñ.
मैं ठीक हूँ।

I'm afraid. Mujhe ḍar lagā.
मुझे डर लगा।

I'm irritated. Maiñ pareshān hūñ.
मैं परेशान हूँ।

Don't irritate me! Merā dimāg mat khāo!
मेरा दिमाग़ मत खाओ !

Literally "Don't eat my brain!"

I'm mad at you. Maiñ tum se nārāz hūñ.
मैं तुम से नाराज़ हूँ ।

I'm pissed off, man! Kitnā baṅkas hai, yār!
कितना बंकस है, यार !

I'm fucked! Maiñ to mar gayā ♂/gayī ♀!
मैं तो मर गया/गयी !

Literally "I've died!" In hip Mumbai-style lingo, you could say **mujhe vāṭ lag gayī**, literally "my death rites are on."

It's all over! Sab khallās ho gayā!
सब ख़ल्लास हो गया !

I'm confused. Maiñ bhram meñ hūñ.
मैं भ्रम में हूँ ।

I'm going crazy. Merā dimāg kharāb ho rahā hai.
मेरा दिमाग़ ख़राब हो रहा है ।

I'm ready.	Maiñ taiyār hūñ. मैं तैयार हूँ ।
I'm tired/exhausted.	Maiñ thak gayā ♂/gayī ♀. मैं थक गया/गयी ।
I'm sleepy.	Mujhe nīnd ā rahī hai. मुझे नींद आ रही है ।

Literally "Sleep is coming to me."

I'm stoned.	Maiñ nashe meñ hūñ. मैं नशे में हूँ ।
I'm drunk/pissed.	Maiñ tallī hūñ. मैं तल्ली हूँ ।
I'm hung over.	Mujhe khumār huā. मुझे खुमार हुआ ।
I feel like hurling/ retching.	Mujhe ulṭī ā rahī hai. मुझे उलटी आ रही है ।
I'm surprised.	Mujhe hairān huā. मुझे हैरान हुआ ।
I'm shocked.	Mujhe shock huā. मुझे शाक हुआ ।

Alternatively, and on a linguistically higher level, **maiñ sadme meñ hūñ.**

I'm dispirited.	Mujhe ūb huī. मुझे ऊब हुई ।
I'm bored with …	Maiñ … se bezār hūñ. मैं ... से बेज़ार हूँ ।
I'm tired of it.	Mujhe kāfī ho gayā. मुझे काफ़ी हो गया ।
What a drag!	Kitnā bekār hai! कितना बेकार है !

What a disaster!	Kyā musībat hai! क्या मुसीबत है।
It's horrible!	Ekdam <u>kh</u>aufnāk hai! एकदम ख़ौफ़नाक है।
What a pity!	Kitnī afsos kī bāt! कितनी अफ़सोस की बात !
What a relief!	Kitnī rāhat hai! कितनी राहत है !
I am ill.	Maiñ bīmār hūñ. मैं बीमार हूँ।
I'm disappointed.	Maiñ nirāsh hūñ. मैं निराश हूँ।
I was worried.	Mujhe cintā huī. मुझे चिंता हुई।
Sorry!	Afsos kī bāt hai. अफ़सोस की बात है।

Note: There's no real "sorry" as an apology in Hindi, Indians being quite sparing with apologies and thanks—informality rules. The above sentence literally means "It's a matter of regret."

I'm sorry that …	Maiñ dukhī hūñ ki … मैं दुःखी हूँ कि …

Literally, "I'm pained that …"

I can't help it.	Maiñ kuch nahīñ kar saktā ♂/ saktī ♀. मैं कुछ नहीं कर सकता/सकती।
That can't be helped.	Koī nikās nahīñ. कोई निकास नहीं।
There's no alternative.	Koī vikalp nahīñ. कोई विकल्प नहीं।

I understand.	Maiñ samajhtā ♂/samajhtī ♀ hūñ. मैं समझता/समझती हूँ ।
I know.	Mujhe patā/mālūm hai. मुझे पता/मालूम है ।
I know him/her.	Maiñ us ko jāntā ♂/jāntī ♀ hūñ. मैं उस को जानता/जानती हूँ ।
I'll think about it.	Maiñ uskā vicār karūñgā ♂/ karūñgī ♀. मैं उसका विचार करूँगा/करूँगी ।
I'll see.	Maiñ dekh lūñgā ♂/lūñgī ♀. मैं देख लूँगा/लूँगी ।
I made a mistake.	Maiñ ne galtī kī. मैं ने ग़लती की ।

Am I right?	Maiñ ne ṭhīk kahā hai, ki (nahīñ)? मैं ने ठीक कहा है, कि (नहीं) ?
Am I wrong?	Maiñ ne galat kahā? मैं ने ग़लत कहा ?

Curses, Insults & Fight Talk 9

Got a problem?	Koī taklīf hai, kyā? कोई तकलीफ़ है, क्या ?
What do you want?	Tum ko kyā maṅgtā hai? तुम को क्या मंगता है ?
Do you want to say something?	Tum ko kuch bolnā maṅgtā hai? तुम को कुछ बोलना मंगता है ?
What are you staring at?	Mujh ko kyā tāk rahe ♂/ rahī ♀ ho? मुझ को क्या ताक रहे/रही हो ?
What did you just say?	Tum ne yah kyā bolā! तुम ने यह क्या बोला !
What's that supposed to mean?	Yah kyā matlab hai? यह क्या मतलब है ?
Don't mess with me!	Mujh se paṅgā mat lenā! मुझ से पंगा मत लेना !
Want to get a little trouble?	Lafṛā maṅgtā, kyā? लफ़ड़ा मंगता, क्या ?
You have a big mouth!	Tumhārī ek lambī zabān hai! तुम्हारी एक लंबी ज़बान है ।

Literally, "You have a long tongue!"

I'll shut your big mouth!	Maiñ tumhārī lambī zabān kāṭūñgā♂/kāṭūñgī♀! मैं तुम्हारी लंबी ज़बान काटूँगा/काटूँगी !

Literally, "I'll cut your long tongue!"

Don't get above yourself!	Tumhārī auḵāt mat bhūlo! तुम्हारी औक़ात मत भूलो !

Literally "Don't forget your low position!" This sentence has been heard in countless Hindi movies; it's part and parcel of many an argument, fictional and otherwise. The sentence reflects in no uncertain terms the Indian caste system and Indian society's strict hierarchical structure. Needless to say, it's not very nice to remind someone of his or her "low" standing in society—but that's what insults are made for, aren't they?

Come here, I'll teach you a lesson!	Yahāñ ā, maiñ tum ko sabak sikhāūñgā!♂/sikhāūñgī♀! यहाँ आ, मैं तुम को सबक़ सिखाऊँगा/सिखाऊँगी !

Note: You could also say, somewhat more colorfully, **Ā jā, maiñ tum ko nānī kī yād dilāūñgā/dilāūñgī!** = "Come here, I'll remind you of your (maternal) grandmother!"

I'll kick the shit out of you!	Maiñ tum ko lāt–lāt mārūñgā♂/mārūñgī♀! मैं तुम को लात-लात माररूँगा/मारूँगी!
I'll finish you off!	Maiñ tum ko zindā nahīñ choṛūñgā♂/choṛūñgī♀! मैं तुम को ज़िंदा नहीं छोड़ूँगा/छोड़ूँगी !

Literally "I won't let you stay alive!", the favorite battle-cry of Indian movie "heroes" and small-time crooks. If you aren't one, use at your own peril.

I'll make you die like a dog! — Maiñ tum ko kutte kī maut dilāūñgā ♂/dilāūñgī ♀!
मैं तुम को कुत्ते की मौत दिलाऊँगा/दिलाऊँगी !

Another standard movie boast. Caution as above.

Stop it! — Yah choṛ do!
यह छोड़ दो !

Shut up! — Mūñh band rakh!
मूंह बंद रख !

Watch your language! — Zabān sambhālke bol!
ज़बान संभालके बोल !

Don't you know about my about my (high) connections? — Tum ko mālūm nahīñ, merī pahūñc kahāñ-kahāñ tak hai?
तुम को मालूम नहीं, मेरी पहूंच कहाँ-कहाँ तक है ?

Boasting about connections in high places is part of many a verbal fight. Some may bluster **Tum ko mālūm nahīñ merā pitā kaun hai?** = "Don't you know who my father is?" Well, a fitting retort would be **Agar tum ko mālūm nahīñ, mujhe kyā patā!** = "If you don't know, how would I know!"

On a side note: **pitā** is the polite word for "father", which anyone would use when talking about their own or any respected person's father. If the intention is to insult someone's father, one uses **bāp**, which could be very loosely translated as "your stupid dirty old man".

Get out of the way! This isn't your private property! — Side meñ jāo, yah tumhāre bāp kī jagah nahīñ!
साइड में जाओ, यह तुम्हारे बाप की जगह नहीं !

Literally "Step aside, this isn't your father's place!"

Don't take it badly! Būrā mat māno!
बूरा मत मानो !

I'll beat you with sandals/shoes. Maiñ tum ko cappaloñ/jūtoñ se mārūñgā ♂/mārūñgī ♀?
मैं तुम को चप्पलों/जूतों से मारूँगा/मारूँगी ?

Note: To beat someone with a piece of footwear may seem an odd idea, but in Indian context it's a serious act of contempt. Shoes are considered low, dirty and spiritually polluted, since they are manufactured from dead animals. A person who has committed a misdemeanor or indecency may be set upon by the aggrieved party and be battered with his or her sandal. Indian stage artists, if performing below expectations, may see shoes hurled in their direction. Obviously, unless having stocked up on some extra missiles beforehand, a section of the audience will have to hobble home barefoot.

I spit on you! Maiñ tum pe thūk rahā ♂/rahī ♀ hūñ!
मैं तुम पे थूक रहा/रही हूँ !

Do you think you're some kind of hero? Apne āp ko hero samajh rahe ho?
अपने आप को हीरो समझ रहे हो ?

He owns you, man! Vah to terā bāp hai, yār!
वह तो तेरा बाप है, यार !

Literally, "He is your father, pal!" If someone is considered your "father", he is obviously regarded as superior, more experienced, or craftier. It also implies he sleeps with your mother.

He's the man! Vah to ustād/guru hai!
वह तो उसताद/गुरु है ।

Literally "He's the master!" **Ustād** or **guru** translate as "master" or "revered teacher". In slang they can denote someone who is clever, crafty, resourceful, skilled, or even slightly criminal.

Don't do it again!	Āindā aisā mat karnā! आइंदा ऐसा मत करना !
Help!	Bacāo! बचाओ !
Have mercy!	Dayā ke li(y)e! दया के लिए !
Leave me alone!/ Let me go!	Mujhe choṛ do! मुझे छोड़ दो !
Don't make me laugh, pal.	Mujhe hañsāo mat, yār. मुझे हंसाओ मत, यार ।
Say you're sorry!	Māfī māṅg lo! माफ़ी मांग लो !
What stupidity!	Kyā bevakūfī! क्या बेवकूफ़ी !
You're crazy!	Tum pāgal ho! तुम पागल हो !
You're nuts!	Tumhārā dimāg <u>kh</u>arāb ho gayā! तुम्हारा दिमाग़ ख़राब हो गया !
Fucking idiot!	Ḍhakkan kahīñ kā! ढक्कन कहीं का !
Smartass!	Ḍeṛh shāne! डेढ़ शाने !
Liar!	Jūṭhā ♂/Jūṭhī ♀! जूठा/जूठी !
Crook/Gangster!	Badmāsh! बदमाश !
You small-time crook!	Taporī kahīñ kā! तपोरी कहीं का !

Pisshead!/ Drunkard!	Bevṛe! बेवड़े !
You bitch!	Kutiyā! कुतिया !
You slut!	Raṇḍī/Chināl! रंडी/छिनाल !
Cunt!	Fuddī! **फुद्दी !**
Low-life dog!	Kutte-kamīne! कुत्ते-कमीने
Son/daughter of a dog!	Kutte kī aulād! कुत्ते की औलाद !
Son/daughter of a sandal-thief!	Cappalcor kī aulād! चप्पलचोर की औलाद !

Note: This is a very Indian insult. Shoes and sandals are considered dirty and unworthy, and anyone stealing them is considered a pathetic little crook (and being the offspring of one is no compliment either). Alternatively, instead of **cappalcor** you could use **cindīcor** = rag-thief, or **kafincor** = coffin-thief.

Bastard!	Harāmzādā ♂/Harāmzādī ♀! हरामज़ादा/हरामज़ादी !

Literally "Illegitimate offspring!" If feeling more verbose, you could ask **Tumhāre māñ-bāp kab shādī kareñge?** = "When will your parents get married?" In Indian view being born out of wedlock is a matter of great shame. Needless to say, your opponent may have some objections at the question.

NAME-CALLING: IT'S A FAMILY AFFAIR!

There are some frequently used insults (**gālī**), which take aim at family relationships and carry sexual innuendo. They have no English equivalents.

साला/साले ! Sālā/sāle! = brother-in-law, to be precise the brother of one's wife. Calling someone sālā or sāle implies that you are married to his sister and have intercourse with her; and that can be construed as a grave insult to her family members. Don't use it lightly.

साली ! Sālī! = Sister-in-law, the sister of one's wife. As above; an insult directed at women.

ससूर / ससूरा ! Sasūr/sasūrā! = Father-in-law, to be precise the father of your wife. An insult directed at men older than the insulter.

One can combine the above with various other swear words. There are countless permutations/combinations. For example:

साला-कुत्ता ! Sālā–kuttā! = Brother-in-law-dog!

साली-कुत्ती ! Sālī–kuttī! = Sister-in-law-bitch!

साला-कुत्ता-कमीना ! Sālā–kuttā–kamīnā! = Brother-in-law-dog-depraved!

साला-कुत्ता-कमीना-हरामज़ादा ! Sālā–kuttā–kamīnā–harāmzādā! = Brother-in-law-dog-depraved-bastard! Etc. Use your imagination. Virtually any combination works.

Limp dick! Hijṛā!
हिजड़ा !

Literally, "Eunuch!"

Wanker! (masturbator) Muṭhal!
मुठल !

Wanker!/Jerk! Cūṭiyā!
चूटिया !

Careful, this is quite a crude word, Literally "from the cunt". Among better company it will certainly produce a jolt.

You cheater/fraud! Cār-sau-bīs!/Dhokhebāz!
चार-सौ-बीस !/धोखेबाज़ !

Literally, "Four hundred twenty." Section 420 of the Indian penal code deals with fraud and cheating; so colloquially, cheaters have become synonymous with this number. The act of cheating or defrauding is called **cār-sau-bisī**. If you get the chance, watch the classic 1955 movie *Shri 420 (Mr. Fraud)*. The title role is played by Raj Kapoor, a legendary actor and director, who modeled himself on Charlie Chaplin.

Pimple-face! Chappan tiklī!
छप्पन तिकली !

Literally, "56 freckles"

Shorty! Ḍeṛh fuṭ!
डेढ़ फ़ुट !

Literally, "One-and-half feet"

Weakling!/Coward! Napuṃsak!
नपुंसक !

Lazy bastard! Kāmcor!/Makhīmār!
कामचोर !/मखीमार !

Note: Makhīmār = Literally, "fly-squasher", an apt description for someone who lazily sprawls on a couch and does nothing but wards off the flies.

Your tool is small! Tumhārā laṇḍ choṭā hai.
तुम्हारा लंड छोटा है ।

Who do you think you are! Tum apne āp ko kyā samajhte ♂/ samajhtī ♀ ho!
तुम अपने आप को क्या समझते/ समझती हो !

Go to hell! Bhāṛ meṅ jāo!
भाड़ में जाओ !

Literally, "Go into the oven!"

Get lost!/Fuck off! Bhāgo!
भागो !

Piss off! Havā āne de!
हवा आने दे !

Literally, "Let air get through!"

Hit the road! Nau-do-gyārah ho jāo!
नौ-दो-ग्यारह हो जाओ !

Literally, "Become nine-two-eleven!" Eleven is a symbol for the two legs, and nine plus two is eleven—so take to your heels and be off!

Just get your ass out of here! Patlī galī se nikal!
पतली गली से निकल !

Away with you! Cal fuṭ!
चल फ़ुट !

Fuck you!

There's no literal translation for this, at least none which would make sense to a Hindi speaker. If you want to curse or insult someone in no uncertain terms you could say, through menacingly clenched teeth, **terī māñ** ... = "your mother ..." The rest is wisely left to the imagination. Simply mentioning your opponent's mother in an angry tone carries a lot of potential insult—the underlying meaning being either "your mother is a whore" or similar pleasantries. Don't use on someone who is obviously stronger than you!

I think you're trying to trick me! Mujhe lagtā hai tum mujh ko cūnā lagā rahe♂/rahī♀ ho!
मुझे लगता है तुम मुझ को चूना लगा रहे/रही हो !

Note: Literally, "I think you're putting lime paste on me." **Cūnā** is a white paste which is added to digestive betel mixtures.

What kind of people do you hang out with? Tumhārā uṭhnā-baiṭhnā kaise logoñ ke sāth hotā hai?
तम्हारा उठना-बैठना कैसे लोगों के साथ होता है ?

Literally "What kind of people do you stand up and sit down with?"

Do you think I'm dumb? Mujhe buddhū samajh rahe♂/rahī♀ ho?
मुझे बुद्धू समझ रहे/रही हो ?

Don't think I'm stupid! Mujhe bevakūf mat samjho!
मुझे बेवक़ूफ मत समझो !

I want to talk to the manager! Mujhe *manager* se bāt karnī cāhi(y)e!
मुझे मैनेजर से बात करनी चाहिए !

I'll never come here again!	Āge idhar kabhī nahīñ āūñgā ♂/ āūñgī ♀! आगे इधर कभी नहीं आऊँगा/ आऊँगी !
I'll tell all my friends!	Maiñ apne sāre dostoñ ko batāūñgā ♂/batāūñgī ♀! मैं अपने सारे दोस्तों को बताऊँगा/बताऊँगी !
OK, you win.	Ṭhīk hai, tum jīt gaye ♂/gayī ♀! ठीक है, तुम जीत गये/गयी !
You're right.	Tum sahī ho. तुम सही हो।
It was my fault.	Merī galtī thī. मेरी ग़लती थी।
Sorry for the trouble!	Māfī mushkil! माफ़ी मुश्किल !
I made a big mistake.	Mujh se baṛī galtī ho gayī. मुझ से बड़ी ग़लती हो गयी।
Forgive me.	Mujhe māf karo. मुझे माफ़ करो।
I forgive you.	Maiñ tum ko māf kartā ♂/ kartī ♀ hūñ. मैं तुम को माफ़ करता/करती हूँ।

Chitchat/ On the Phone 10

Hello.	Helo. हेलो ।
Who is this?	Vah kaun bol rahā ♂/rahī ♀ hai? वह कौन बोल रहा/रही है ?
It's me, John.	Maiñ John bol rahā hūñ. मैं जॉन बोल रहा हूँ ।
It's me, Jane.	Maiñ Jane bol rahī hūñ. मैं जेन बोल रही हूँ ।
What are you doing?	Tum kyā kar rahe ♂/rahī ♀ ho? तुम क्या कर रहे/रही हो ?
Are you free?	Ṭāim hai, kyā? टाइम है, क्या ?
I'm free.	Ṭāim hai. टाइम है ।

Where are you?	Tum kahāñ ho? तुम कहाँ हो ?
I am at home.	Maiñ ghar pe hūñ. मैं घर पे हूँ ।
Shall we meet?	Mileñ? मिलें ?
Do you want to meet?	Milnā cāhi(y)e? मिलना चाहिए ?
Do you want to go out?	Kahīñ jānā cāhte♂/cāhtī♀ ho? कहीं जाना चाहते/चाहती हो ?
Do you want to go to the movie?	*Movie* dekhnā cāhte♂/cāhtī♀ ho? मूवी देखना चाहते/चाहती हो ?
Do you want to go for a little walk?	Ṭhoṛī-sī sair kareñ? थोड़ी-सी सैर करें ?
I want to see you.	Maiñ tum se milnā cāhtā♂/cāhtī♀ hūñ. मैं तुम से मिलना चाहता/चाहती हूँ ।
Mary at home?	Mary ghar par hai? मैरी घर पर है ?
Hold on please.	Ṭhahari(y)e. ठहरिए ।
Mary, telephone!	Mary, tumhārā fon! मैरी, तुम्हारा फ़ोन !
Yes, please!	Farmā(y)e!/Boli(y)e! फ़रमाए !/बोलिए !

Note: Both **Farmā(y)e!** and **Boli(y)e!** can literally be translated as "Please speak!"

Mary is out.	Mary bāhar gayī hai. मैरी बाहर गयी है।
Please tell her ...	Usko boli(y)e ki ... ne fon kiyā. उसको बोलिए कि ... ने फ़ोन किया।
This is Robert.	Maiñ Robert bol rahā hūñ. मैं रॉबेर्ट बोल रहा हूँ।
Are you doing okay?	Hāl–cāl ṭhīk–ṭhāk hai? हाल-चाल ठीक-ठाक है ?
What have you been doing?	Tum kyā kar rahe the ♂/ rahī ♀ thī? तुम क्या कर रहे थे/रही थी ?
Do you have something to write with?	Koī likhne kī cīz hai, kyā? कोई लिखने की चीज़ है, क्या ?
See you later.	Phir mileñge. फिर मिलेंगे।
See you tomorrow.	Kal mileñge. कल मिलेंगे।
I'll call you tomorrow.	Maiñ tum ko kal fon karūñgā ♂/ karūñgī ♀. मैं तुम को कल फ़ोन करूँगा/करूँगी।
Bye!	Bye! बई !

Note: There's no real "Bye!" in Hindi, most modern folk would simply use the English word. Or, one might say, quite informally, **ṭhīk hai, maiñ caltā/caltī hūñ** = "OK, I'll be off then." The formal word would be **namaste!**, which is a form of greeting as well as valediction.

CELLPHONITIS

Cell phones are ubiquitous in India today. There's no proper Hindi word for them, they're simply called *cell phone* or *mobile*. The indispensible little gadgets even render themselves to insults: ***binā signal kā mobile***—literally, cell phone/mobile without signal = idiot, dumbo, dimwit. If you happen to hang out in shady, criminal company you may hear the word **kauvā** (crow) for a cell phone. A mobile is a gangster's second-best friend—his best being his ***ghoṛā*** (horse) or pistol.

Keep it short, my battery is almost gone.	Jaldī karo, merī baiṭrī khatam hone-vālī hai. जल्दी करो, मेरी बैटरी ख़तम होने-वाली है।
Send me an SMS/ Voicemail?	Mujhe SMS/voicemail bhejo. मुझे SMS/voicemail भेजो।
Did you get my SMS/ Voicemail?	Merī SMS/voicemail mil ga(y)ī? मेरी SMS/voicemail मिल गयी ?
I got your SMS/ voicemail.	Tumhārī SMS/voicemail mil ga(y)ī. तुम्हारी SMS/voicemail मिल गयी।
The signal is weak.	Signal kamzor hai. सिगनल कमज़ोर है।
There's no signal here.	Yahāñ pe koī signal nahīñ. यहाँ पे कोई सिगनल नहीं।
My mobile is switched off.	Merā mobile band hai. मेरा मोबाइल बंद है।
Switch your mobile off.	Apnā mobile band karo. अपना मोबाइल बंद करो।

Your mobile is ringing, do answer/take the call.
Tumhārā mobile baj rahā hai, uṭhā lo!
तुम्हारा मोबाइल बज रहा है, उठा लो !

Where can I get a refill/top-up card for my (pre-paid) mobile?
Mobile kā refill card kahāñ milegā?
मोबाइल का रीफ़िल कार्ड कहाँ मिलेगा ?

Making Friends/ Party Talk 11

When meeting people for the first time, it is safer to use a more formal, elegant Hindi—after all, you want to make a good first impression, don't you...

Having a good time?	Mazā ā rahā hai? मज़ा आ रहा है ?
You look like you're having fun.	Lagtā hai ki tum ko mazā ā rahā hai. लगता है कि तुम को मज़ा आ रहा है !
Yeah, I'm having fun.	Hāñ, mazā ā rahā hai! हाँ, मज़ा आ रहा है !
You come here often?	Āp yahāñ barābar āte♂/atī♀ haiñ? आप यहाँ बराबर आते/आती हैं ?
Are you by yourself?	Tum akele āye♂/akelī āyī ho♀? तुम अकेले आये/अकेली आयी हो ?
Yes, I'm here alone.	Jī hāñ, maiñ akelā āyā♂/akelī āyī♀. जी हाँ, मैं अकेला आया/अकेली आयी ।

No, I'm here with my friends.	Jī nahīñ, maiñ apne dostoñ ke sāth āyā♂/āyī♀. जी नहीं, मैं अपने दोस्तों के साथ आया/आयी ।

Note: "Yes" is usually **hāñ**, "no" is **nahīñ**. If you want to leave a good impression, be extra-polite and say **jī hāñ** or **jī nahīñ** respectively. **Jī** is a kind of "politeness particle" which can also be added to names: **Peter-jī** = my dear, beloved Peter; **Sunītā-jī** = my dear, beloved Sunita, etc.

No, I'm here with my husband/wife.	Jī nahīñ, maiñ apne pati ke sāth āyī♂/apnī bīvī ke sāth āyā♀. जी नहीं, मैं अपने पति के साथ आयी/अपनी बीवी के साथ आया ।
Are you married?	Āp shādī-shudā haiñ? आप शादी-शुदा हैं ?

Alternatively, some people would ask, somewhat less sophisticated, **āpkī shādī ho gayī?** = "Has your wedding happened?"

Yes, I'm married.	Jī hāñ, maiñ shādī-shudā hūñ. जी हाँ, मैं शादी-शुदा हूँ ।

Note: Or, **merī shādī ho gayī** = "My wedding has happened."

No, I'm not married.	Jī nahīñ, maiñ shādī-shudā nahīñ. जी नहीं, मैं शादी-शुदा नहीं ।
I'm engaged.	Merī maṅgnī ho gayī. मेरी मँगनी हो गयी ।
May I introduce to you, this is my fiancé/fianceé.	Āp in se mileñ, yah merā♂/merī♀ maṅgetar. आप इन से मिलें, यह मेरा/मेरी मंगेतर ।

Did you two come here together?	Āp donoñ ek sāth āye? आप दोनों एक साथ आये ?
May I join you?	Maiñ āp ke pās baiṭh saktā♂/ saktī♀ hūñ? मैं आप के पास बैठ सकता/सकती हूँ ?
Can I sit here?	Maiñ yahāñ baiṭh saktā♂/ saktī♀ hūñ? मैं यहाँ बैठ सकता/सकती हूँ ?
Please sit down!	Kripayā, baiṭhi(y)e! कृपया बैठिए !
Scoot over.	Side meñ jāo! साइड में जाओ !
Have I seen you before?	Maiñ ne āp ko kahīñ dekhā? मैं ने आप को कहीं देखा ?
You're so beautiful.	Āp behad sundar haiñ. आप बेहद सुंदर हैं ।
You're handsome.	Āp khūbsūrat haiñ. आप ख़ूबसूरत हैं ।
Would you like to sit down?	Āp ko baiṭhnā cāhi(y)e? आप को बैठना चाहिए ?
What's your name?	Āpkā nām kyā hai? आपका नाम क्या है ?
My name is …	Merā nām … hai. मेरा नाम … है ।
What was your name again?	Āpkā nām kyā thā? आपका नाम क्या था ?

Hi, pleased to meet you.	Hi, āp se milne se bahut <u>kh</u>ushī huī हाई, आप से मिलने से बहुत ख़ुशी हुई।

What did you say?	Āp kyā bole ♂/bolīñ ♀? आप क्या बोले/बोलीं ?
Is someone sitting here?	Kyā, yahāñ koī baiṭhā hai? क्या, यहाँ कोई बैठा है ?
Please have a seat!	Baiṭhi(y)e! बैठिए !
Sorry, this seat is taken.	Māf kījiye, yah jagah khālī nahīñ. माफ़ कीजिए, यह जगह ख़ाली नहीं।
Where are you from?	Āp kahāñ se āye ♂/āyīñ ♀? आप कहाँ से आये/आयीं ?
I'm from ...	Maiñ ... se āyā ♂/āyī ♀. मैं ... से आया/आयी।

Where do you live?	Āp kahāñ rahte ♂/rahtī ♀ haiñ? आप कहाँ रहते/रहती हैं ?
I live in ...	Maiñ ... meñ rahtā ♂/rahtī ♀ hūñ. मैं ... में रहता/रहती हूँ ।
Have you been here long?	Yahāñ bahut der se haiñ? यहाँ बहुक देर से हैं ?
A few days.	Kaī din. कई दिन ।
How long will you stay here?	Yahāñ kab tak raheñge ♂/raheñgī ♀? यहाँ कब तक रहेंगे/रहेंगी ?
Where are you staying?	Āp kahāñ ṭhahar rahe ♂/rahī ♀ haiñ? आप कहाँ ठहर रहे/रही हैं ?
I'm staying in a hotel.	Maiñ (ek) hoṭal meñ ṭhahar rahā ♂/rahī ♀ hūñ. मैं (एक) होटल में ठहर रहा/रही हूँ ।
I'm staying with friends.	Maiñ dostoñ ke sāth ṭhahar rahā ♂/rahī ♀ hūñ. मैं दोस्तों के साथ ठहर रहा/रही हूँ ।
How long have you been in India?	Āp Bhārat/India meñ kab se haiñ? आप भारत/इंडिया में कब से हैं ?
Do you like India?	Āp ko Bhārat/India pasand hai? आप को भारत/इंडिया पसंद है ?

Note: "India" is a word invented by foreigners, derived from the name of the river Sindhu, which is also the root of the word "Hindu." The official Hindi name for the country is **Bhārat**.

How old are you?	Āpkī umar kitnī hai? आपकी उमर कितनी है ?

I'm ... years old.	Maiñ ... sāl kā♂/kī♀ hūñ. मैं ... साल का/की हूँ।

Literally "I'm of ... years."

Do you have a steady boyfriend/ girlfriend?	Tumhāre pās pakkā *boyfriend*/ pakkī *girlfriend* hai? तुम्हारे पास पक्का बोयफ़्रैंड/ पक्की गर्लफ़्रैंड है ?
I'm single.	Maiñ single hūñ. मैं सिंगल हूँ।

There's a proper Hindi word for single, **avivāhit**, but it's too formal for casual conversations.

I'm married.	Maiñ shādī–shudā/vivāhit hūñ. मैं शादी-शुदा/विवाहित हूँ।

Note: Shādī–shudā is fine in conversations, **vivāhit** on the other hand may sound a bit too formal or pompous.

I'm separated.	Maiñ alag rah rahā♂/rahī♀ hūñ. मैं अलग रह रहा/रही हूँ।
I'm divorced.	Merī *divorce* ho gayī. मेरी डिवॉर्स हो गयी।

Note: A couple of decades ago, the word divorce wouldn't have found its way into a Hindi phrasebook. Divorces used to be almost unheard of in India. Today though, mores are changing, especially in the major metropolises. There is a formal Hindi word for divorce, **vivāh–vicched** (marriage-severing), but it sounds too high-falutin' to be used in everyday speech.

I live alone.	Maiñ akelā rahtā♂/akelī♀ rahtī hūñ. मैं अकेला रहता/अकेली रहती हूँ।

I live with someone. Maiñ kisī ke sāth rahtā♂/rahtī♀ hūñ.
मैं किसी के साथ रहता/रहती हूँ ।

In villages, premarital cohabitation is virtually impossible and could lead to violent confrontations with parents and village elders. In the large metropolises though, a few modern and well-to-do unwed couples do shack up together.

Who's all living in your house(hold)? Tumhāre ghar meñ kaun–kaun rahtā hai?
तुम्हारे घर में कौन-कौन रहता है ?

Note: The majority of Indians live in joint families or **samyukt parivār**. If the target of your romantic attention doesn't, lucky you: the odds of getting anywhere are much higher. The answer, though, might well be "I live with my parents, two brothers, one sister, my grandmother, an uncle, and my orphaned nephew".

Do you live with your parents? Tum apne māñ–bāp ke sāth rahte♂/rahtī♀ ho?
तुम अपने माँ-बाप के साथ रहते/रहती हो ?

Note: As seen elsewhere, the word **bāp** "father" is usually an insult. In the combination with **māñ** "mother", though, it's perfectly OK: **māñ–bāp** = "parents."

That's none of your business. Us se tumhārā koī len–den nahīñ.
उस से तुम्हारा कोई लेन-देन नहीं ।

Are you a student? Āp *student* haiñ?
आप स्टूडेंट हैं ?

The proper words for student, **vidyārthī** (m)/**vidyārthinī** (f), would hardly be used colloquially.

Your English is good. Āp aṅgrezī acchī tarah se bol rahe/rahī haiñ.
आप अंग्रज़ी अच्छी तरह से बोल रहे/रही हैं ।

Literally "You are speaking English well."

What's your job?	Āp kyā kām karte ♂/kartī ♀ haiñ? आप क्या काम करते/करती हैं ?
That's an interesting job.	Yah ek dilcasp kām hai. यह एक दिलचस्प काम है।
Do you like your job?	Āp apne kām se santuṣṭ haiñ? आप अपने काम से संतुष्ट हैं ?
Most of the time./ Generally.	Aksar. अक्सर।
Where do you work?	Āp kahāñ kām kar rahe ♂/ rahī ♀ haiñ? आप कहाँ काम कर रहे/रही हैं ?
What hobbies do you have?	Āpkī kaunsī hobbies haiñ? आपकी कौनसी हॉबिज़ हैं ?
I like …	Mujhe … pasand hai. मुझे … पसंद है।

Insert any of the following nouns:

movies	*movies*, filam मूविज़, फ़िलम

Note that the "a" in film is very short, sometimes almost imperceptible.

watching TV	*TV* dekhnā टी वी देखना
sports	*sports*, khelkūd स्पॉर्टस, खेलकूद
tennis	*tennis* टेनिस
swimming	tairnā, *swimming* तैरना

golf	*golf* गोल्फ़
soccer	*football, soccer* फ़ुटबॉल, सॉकर
jogging	*jogging* जॉगिंग
dancing	nācnā, *dancing* नाचना
exercise	*exercise*, kasrat कसरत
going for a walk	sair karnā सैर करना
cycling	*cycle* karnā सायकल करना
music	*music*, saṅgīt संगीत
travel	*travel*, safar karnā सफ़र करना
reading	paṛhnā पढ़ना
reading magazines/ newspapers/ books	patrikāeñ/samācārpatra/ kitābeñ paṛhnā पत्रिकाएं/समाचारपत्र/किताबें पढ़ना

Note: These three nouns may sound too formal to some Hindi speakers. You can easily replace them with their English equivalents and just add **paṛhnā** "to read."

studies	paṛhāī पढ़ाई

relaxing	ārām karnā आराम करना
sleeping	sonā सोना
lazing around doing nothing	lukhāgirī karnā लुखागिरी करना
What music do you like?	Kis tarah kī *music*/ke gāne pasand karte ♂/kartī ♀ ho? किस तरह की म्यूज़िक/के गाने पसंद करते/करती हो ?

I like rock music.	Mujhe *rock music* pasand hai. मुझे रॉक म्यूज़िक पसंद है।
I like Indian classical music.	Mujhe shāstrīya saṅgīt pasand hai. मुझे शास्त्रीय संगीत पसंद है।
You know this song?	Is *song*/gīt ko pahcānte ♂/pahcāntī ♀ ho? इस सँग/गीत को पहचानते/पहचानती हो ?

Where else do you go to dance?	Nācne ke li(y)e tum aur kahāñ jāte♂/jātī♀ ho? नाचने के लिए तुम और कहाँ जाते/जाती हो ?
Wanna dance?	Nāceñ? नाचें ?
I can't dance.	Maiñ nāc nahīñ saktā♂/saktī♀. मैं नाच नहीं सकता/सकती ।
Are you in the mood?	Man lagtā hai? मन लगता है ?
I'm not in the mood.	Mujhe man nahīñ lag rahā hai. मुझे मन नहीं लग रहा है ।
You dance well.	Tum acchī tarah se nāc rahe/rahī ho. तुम अच्छी तरह से नाच रहे/रही हो ।
Do you want to go somewhere else?	Kahīñ āge caleñ? कहीं आगे चलें ?
Where shall we go?	Kahāñ jāyeñ? कहाँ जायें ?

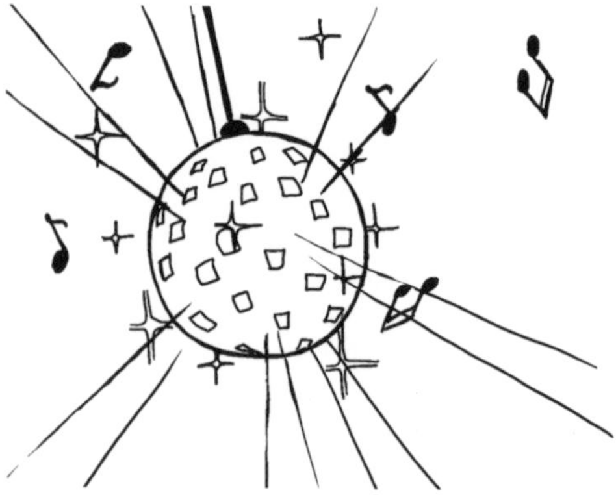

What are you drinking?	Tum kyā pī rahe ♂/rahī ♀ ho? तुम क्या पी रहे/रही हो ?
This is my first (second) drink.	Yah merī pahlī (dūsrī) *drink* hai. यह मेरी पहली (दूसरी) ड्रिंक है।
One small shot, please!	Ek choṭā peg dījiye! एक छोटा पैग दीजिए !
Put some ice in!	Baraf ḍālo! बरफ़ डालो !
I don't want ice.	Mujhe baraf nahīñ cāhi(y)e. मुझे बरफ़ नहीं चाहिए।
Can I buy you a drink?	Tum ko kuch pilāūñ? तुम को कुछ पिलाऊँ।
What would you like to drink?	Tum kyā pīnā cāhte ♂/cāhtī ♀ ho? तुम क्या पीना चाहते/चाहती हो ?
Would you like a cigarette/cigar?	Tum ko *cigarette*/cigar cāhi(y)e? तुम को सिगरेट/सिगार चाहिए ?

In slang, you could say **suttā cāhi(y)e? or suttā maṅgtā? Suttā** can be anything smokable, cigarette, cigar, or beedi, the traditional Indian cigarette.

Do you have a light?	Mācis hai? माचिस है ?
Have you been drinking a lot?	Tum ne bahut piyā? तुम ने बहुत पिया ?
Are you drunk?	Tallī ho? तल्ली हो ?

To impress your co-guzzlers you could quote a line from famous movie Naseeb (1981), in which "hero" Amitabh Bachchan drunkenly intones: **Jiskā baṛā bhāī ho sharābī, choṭe pīye to kyā <u>kh</u>arābī** = When your elder brother is a drunkard, why can't the younger brother get drunk/smashed, too. If you get the monologue right, your next free drink may be secured.

Are you OK?	Tum ṭhīk ho? तुम ठीक हो ?
I think you've had enough.	Mere khayāl se tum se kāfī pī gayā. मेरे ख़याल से तुम से काफ़ी पी गया ।
Maybe you should stop drinking.	Shāyad tum ko pīnā band karnā cāhi(y)e. शायद तुम को पीना बंद करना चाहिए ।
What time did you come here?	Tum kitne baje yahāñ par āye ♂/āyī ♀? तुम कितने बजे यहाँ पर आये/आयी ?
When do you have to be back home?	Tum ko kitne baje ghar par lauṭnā hai? तुम को कितने बजे घर पर लौटना है ?
What time are you leaving?	Kitne baje vāpas jāoge ♂/jāogī ♀? कितने बजे वापस जाओगे/जाओगी ?
It depends/ Let's see.	Dekhnā paṛegā. देखना पड़ेगा ।
Don't go yet.	Abhī mat jāo. अभी मत जाओ ।
Let's have a good time!	Calo, mauj–mastī kareñ! चलो, मौज-मस्ती करें !
What shall we do?	Kyā kareñ? क्या करें ?
Shall we leave?	Calnā, kyā? चलना, क्या ?

Note: Alternatively you could say, Mumbai hipster-style, **Kaltī māreñ?** or **Fuṭ leñ?** = "Shall we bugger off?"

Shall we go somewhere else?	Koī dūsrī jagah jāeñ, kyā? कोई दूसरी जगह जाएं, क्या ?
Shall we go for a walk/round?	Ghūmne/cakkar mārne kā man lagtā hai? घूमने/चक्कर मारने का मन लगता है ?
Shall we get some air?	Havā khāne kā man lagtā hai? हवा खाने का मन लगता है ?

Note: Literally "Do you feel like eating air?" In Hindi, you can also "eat the heat" (**dhūp khānā**), which actually means "to take a sunbath."

Shall we go for a drive?	Gāṛī se cakkar māreñ, kyā? गाड़ी से चक्कर मारें, क्या ?
Yes, all right.	Hāñ, ṭhīk hai. हाँ, ठीक है ।
No, thank you.	Jī nahīñ. जी नहीं ।
I don't feel like it.	Man nahīñ lagtā. मन नहीं लगता ।
Can/shall my friends come?	Mere dost bhī āyeñ? मेरे दोस्त भी आयें ?
Where shall we go?	Kahāñ jāeñ? कहाँ जाएं?
What shall we do?	Kyā kareñ? क्या करें ?
It's up to you.	Tumhārī marzī. तुम्हारी मरज़ी ।
I'd like to stay here longer.	Maiñ yahāñ pe aur rahnā cāhtā ♂/ cāhtī ♀ hūñ. मैं यहाँ पे और रहना चाहता/ चाहती हूँ ।

I'll take you home.	Maiñ tum ko ghar pe pahuñcāūñgā ♂/ pahuñcāūñgī ♀. मैं तुम को घर पे पहुंचाऊँगा/ पहुंचाऊँगी ।
Do you want to come to my place?	Mere ghar jānā cāhte ♂/cāhtī ♀ ho? मेरे घर जाना चाहते/चाहती हो ?
I'm not sure.	Patā nahīñ. पता नहीं ।
Just for a drink.	Kuch pīne ke li(y)e. कुछ पीने के लिए ।
Just for coffee.	*Coffee* pīne ke li(y)e. कॉफ़ी पीने के लिए ।
Goodbye.	Phir mileñge. फिर मिलेंगे ।
Goodnight.	Shubh rātri. शुभ रात्रि ।

Getting Serious 12

I want to know more about you.	Maiñ tum se aur kuch jānnā cāhtā♂/cāhtī♀ hūñ. मैं तुम से और कुछ जानना चाहता/चाहती हूँ।
I want to know all about you.	Maiñ tumhāre♂/tumhārī♀ bāre meñ sab kuch jānnā cāhtā♂/cāhtī♀ hūñ. मैं तुम्हारे/तुम्हारी बारे में सब कुछ जानना चाहता/चाहती हूँ।
I'll tell you.	Maiñ tum ko batāūñgā♂/batāūñgī♀. मैं तुम को बताऊँगा/बताऊँगी।
Shall we meet again?	Phir se mileñ? फिर से मिलें ?
Are you free tonight?	Āj shām fursat hai? आज शाम फ़ुरसत है ?
Are you free over the weekend?	Āne–vāle shanivār–ravivār fursat hai? आने-वाले शनिवार-रविवार फ़ुरसत है ?
Would you like to go out with me?	Mere sāth kahīñ jāeñ, kyā? मेरे साथ कहीं जाएं, क्या ?
I already have a boyfriend.	Merā (ek) *boyfriend*/hai. मेरा (एक) बोयफ़्रैंड है।

I already have a girlfriend.	Merī (ek) *girlfriend* hai. मेरी (एक) गर्लफ़्रैंड है।
When can I see you next time?	Phir se tum se kab mil sakūñgā♂/sakūñgī♀? फिर से तुम से कब मिल सकूँगा/सकूँगी ?
Do you have any plans for tonight?	Is shām ke li(y)e kuch khās plan hai, kyā? इस शाम के लिए कुछ ख़ास प्लैन है, क्या ?
I already have a date.	Kisī aur se milnā hai. किसी और से मिलना है।
Where shall we meet?	Kahāñ par mileñ? कहाँ पर मिलें ?
May I call you?	Maiñ tum ko fon karūñ? मैं तुम को फ़ोन करूँ ?
May I have your phone number?	Kripā karke, mujhe apnī fon nambar doge♂/dogī♀? कृपा करके, मुझे अपनी फ़ोन नंबर दोगे/दोगी ?
Here's my phone number.	Lo, merī nambar. लो, मेरी नंबर।
Will you call me?	Mujhe fon karoge♂/karogī♀? मुझे फ़ोन करोगे/करोगी ?
You're very nice.	Tum bahut pyāre♂/pyārī♀ ho. तुम बहुत प्यारे/प्यारी हो।
I enjoyed myself.	Mujhe mazā āyā. मुझे मज़ा आया।
It was fun.	Mazā āyā. मज़ा आया।

I like being with you.	Tumhārā sāth denā mujhe pasand hai. तम्हारा साथ देना मुझे पसंद है ।।
I've missed you.	Mujhe tumhārī yād ātī thī. मुझे तुम्हारी याद आती थी ।
I dreamed about you.	Maiñ ne tumhārā sapnā dekhā. मैं ने तुम्हारा सपना देखा ।
I've been thinking of you.	Tum mujhe hameshā yād āye/āyīñ. तुम मुझे हमेशा याद आये/आयीं ।
Will you pick me up?	Tum mujhe lene āoge ♂/āogī ♀? तुम मुझे लेने आओगे/आओगी ?
Shall I pick you up?	Maiñ tum ko lene āūñ? मैं तुम को लेने आऊँ ?
I can't go out now.	Maiñ is vak̲t bāhar nahīñ jā saktā ♂/saktī ♀ hūñ. मैं इस वक़्त बाहर नहीं जा सकता/सकती हूँ ।
I have to be home by …	Mujhe … baje ghar pe lauṭnā hai. मुझे … बजे घर पे लौटना है ।
I'll call you again.	Maiñ tum ko phir se fon karūñgā ♂/karūñgī ♀. मैं तुम को फिर से फ़ोन करूँगा/करूँगी ।
I'll write you a letter/ an e-mail.	Maiñ tum ko ciṭṭhī/*e-mail* bhejūñgā ♂/bhejūñgī ♀. मैं तुम को चिट्ठी/ई-मेल भेजूँगा/भेजूँगी ।

Will you write me a letter/ an e-mail?
Mujhe ciṭṭhī/*e-mail* bhejoge♂/ bhejogī♀?
मुझे चिट्ठी/ई-मेल भेजोगे/भेजोगी ?

I'll call you from America.
Maiñ tum ko America se fon karūñgā♂/karūñgī♀.
मैं तुम को अमेरीका से फ़ोन करूँगा/ करूँगी ।

I'll call you when I return (here).
Lauṭ āke tum ko fon karūñgā♂/ karūñgī♀.
लौट आके तुम को फ़ोन करूँगा/ करूँगी ।

Promise?
Vādā?
वादा ?

When will you be back?
Tum kab vāpas āoge♂/āogī♀?
तुम कब वापस आओगे/आओगी ?

I'll be back soon.
Maiñ jaldī vāpas āūñgā♂/āūñgī♀.
मैं जल्दी वापस आऊँगा/आऊँगी ।

Do you have to go?
Tum ko jānā paṛegā?
तुम को जाना पड़ेगा ?

Note: The verb "to have to" or "must" is rendered in three different ways in Hindi: **Tum ko jānā paṛegā?, Tum ko jānā hai?** or **Tum ko jānā cāhi(y)e?** However, each of these sentences reflects a particular situation. The first sentence implies that there is an obligation from a third party, the second includes a temporal factor, i.e. that the obligation will take place in the future, and only the third one is of general nature.

Please don't go!
Mat jāyā karo!
मत जाया करो !

Stay here with me!
Mere pās raho!
मेरे पास रहो !

Please understand.	Zarā samjho! ज़रा समझो !
Take care of your health.	Apnā <u>kh</u>ayāl rakho. अपना ख़याल रखो ।

Note: This sentence simply means "Take care." Other such farewells include **<u>Kh</u>ush raho!** "Stay happy!", **Jīte raho!** "Stay alive!" or **Salāmat raho!** "May you remain safe!"

Please wait for my return.	Kripā karke, merī vāpasī kā intazār karo. कृपा करके, मेरी वापसी का इंतज़ार करो ।

Note: Instead of the somewhat wordy **kripā karke** many people simply say "please."

Wait for me.	Merā intazār karo! मेरा इंतज़ार करो !
Don't cry.	Ronā mat. रोना मत ।

I won't be able to forget you.	Maiñ tum ko bhulā nahīñ pāūñgā ♂/pāūñgī ♀. मैं तुम को भुला नहीं पाऊँगा/पाऊँगी।
I'll be waiting for you.	Maiñ tumhārā intazār karūñgā ♂/karūñgī ♀. मैं तम्हारा इंतज़ार करूँगा/करूँगी।

Love & Sex 13

I love you. Maiñ tum ko pyār kartā♂/ kartī♀ hūñ.
मैं तुम को प्यार करता/करती हूँ ।

Note: It literally translates as "I make love to you" but it's not meant in any physical way. Alternatively one could say: **Mujhe tum se pyār hai.**

Hindi has a good array of synonyms for love: **pyār**, **muhabbat/ mohabbat**, **ishk**, **prem**. Yet, colloquially only **pyār** and (less so) **muhabbat** are used.

I'm in love with you. Mujhe tum se pyār ho gayā.
मुझे तुम से प्यार हो गया ।

I'm in love with you, too. Mujhe bhī tum se pyār ho gayā.
मुझे भी तुम से प्यार हो गया।

I'm fond of you. Tum mujhe acche lagte ♂/acchī lagtī ♀ ho.
तुम मुझे अच्छे लगते/अच्छी लगती हो।

Don't suppress your feelings! Apnā dil choṭā mat karo!
अपना दिल छोटा मत करो!

Literally "Don't make your heart small!"

I don't feel that way about you. Tere–mere jazbāt barābar nahīñ.
तेरे-मेरे जज़बात बराबर नहीं।

I'm crazy about you! Maiñ tujh pe martā ♂/ martī ♀ hūñ.
मैं तुझ पे मरता/मरती हूँ।

Note: This sentence literally means: "I die over you."

I'm yours. Maiñ tumhārā ♂/tumhārī ♀ hūñ.
मैं तुम्हारा/तुम्हारी हूँ।

You're mine. Tum mere ♂/merī ♀ ho.
तुम मेरे/मेरी हो।

You're beautiful. Tum sundar ho.
तुम सुंदर हो।

You're attractive. Tum attractive ho.
तुम अट्रेक्टिव हो।

Note: Well, or just stop beating around the bush and say "sexy" instead of "attractive." The word "sexy" made its major Indian entry in the 1990s, and it was quickly picked up for a silly film song with the title "Merī Paiṇṭ Bhī Sexy" ("Even My Pants Are Sexy").

You have such a sweet smile. Tumhārī muskarāhaṭ bahut hī mīṭhī hai.
तुम्हारी मुसकराहट बहुत ही मीठी है।

You have beautiful breasts/eyes.	Tumhārī sundar chātī/āṅkheñ haiñ. तुम्हारी सुंदर छाती/आँखें हैं।
You have beautiful hands/legs/lips/teeth.	Tumhāre sundar hāth/pair/hoṇṭh/dānt haiñ. तुम्हारे सुंदर हाथ/पैर/होंठ/दाँत हैं।
You're a pretty boy!	Ciknā hai tū! चिकना है तू !
You're a pretty doll!	Ciknī hai tū! चिकनी है तू !
Hey good-looking!	He cikne ♂/ciknī ♀! हे चिकने/चिकनी !
Your nose is lovely.	Tumhārī nāk khūbsūrat hai. तुम्हारी नाक ख़ूबसूरत है।
You have a beautiful body.	Tumhārī body sundar hai. तुम्हारी बौडी सुंदर है।

Note: Hindi has several synonyms for "body"—**sharīr, tan, badan, jism**—but they wouldn't quite fit the situation.

You smell sweet.	Tum se <u>kh</u>ushbū ātī hai. तुम से ख़ुशबू आती है।
May I kiss you?	Maiñ tum ko cummā de saktā ♂/saktī ♀ hūñ? मैं तुम को चुम्मा दे सकता/सकती हूँ ?
Kiss me.	Mujhe cummā do. मुझे चुम्मा दो।
I want to hold your hand.	Maiñ tumhārā hāth pakaṛnā cāhtā ♂/cāhtī ♀ hūñ. मैं तुम्हारा हाथ पकड़ना चाहता/चाहती हूँ।

Note: Speaking of "I Want to Hold Your Hand", search on Youtube for the song "Dekho Ab To" ("Have a Look Now") from the movie *Janwar* (1964), which is the Hindi version of the old Beatles hit. We guarantee you'll have a good laugh!

Come closer to me!	Mere nazdīk āo! मेरे नज़दीक आओ !
Hug me.	Mujhe jhappī do. मुझे झप्पी दो ।
I don't want to rush into it.	Mujhe jaldī karnā nahīñ cāhi(y)e. मुझे जल्दी करना नहीं चाहिए ।
Do you want to have sex?	Mujh se sambhog karnā cāhte♂/cāhtī♀ ho? मुझ से संभोग करना चाहते/चाहती हो ?

Note: This is quite a respectful question, **sambhog** translating as "intercourse": "Do you wish sexual intercourse with me?". To be much more direct, and/or in roughshod company, you could say **codnā/pelnā/ṭhoknā mangtā**? "Wanna fuck?"

Otherwise, as a man, you can ask a woman: **Degī**? = Will you give it to me/do it with me?

A woman on the other hand could ask: **Lagāoge**? = Will you put in on me/give it to me?

Will you spend the night with me?	Mujh se rāt bitāoge♂/bitāogī♀? मुझ से रात बिताओगे/बिताओगी ?
I'm embarrassed.	Mujhe sharm ā rahī hai. मुझे शर्म आ रही है ।

Don't be shy.	Sharmāo mat. शर्माओ मत ।
Close your eyes.	Apnī aṅkheñ band karo. अपनी अँखें बंद करो ।
Turn off the light.	Bijlī band karo. बिजली बंद करो ।?
Is this your first time?	Yah tumhārī pahlī bār hai? यह तुम्हारी पहली बार है ?
Tell me the truth.	Sac batāo. सच बताओ ।
I am still a virgin.	Maiñ kumārī hūñ. मैं कुमारी हूँ ।
I'm frightened.	Mujhe ḍar lagā. मुझे डर लगा ।
Don't worry.	Fikr/Cintā mat karo. फ़िक्र/चिंता मत करो ।

It's going to be OK.	Sab ṭhīk hogā. सब ठीक होगा ।
I'll be careful.	Maiñ āhistā kar dūñgā♂/ dūñgī♀. मैं आहिस्ता कर दूँगा/दूँगी ।
I'm afraid I'll get pregnant.	Mujhe garbhvatī hone kī cintā hai. मुझे गर्भवती होने की चिंता है ।
We shouldn't take any risks.	Koī jhokim nahīñ lenā hai. कोई झोकिम नहीं लेना है ।
Will you use protection?	Koī surakshā istemāl karoge♂/ karogī♀? कोई सुरक्षा इस्तेमाल करोगे/ करोगी ?
Only if we use a condom.	Sirf kāṇḍam lagāke. सिर्फ़ काँडम लगाके ।
Do you have a condom?	Tumhāre pās kāṇḍam hai? तुम्हारे पास काँडम है ?
Are you on the pill?	Tum garbh-nirodhak golī khā rahī ho? तुम गर्भ-निरोधक गोली खा रही हो ?

Note: Garbh-nirodhak golī = anti-pregnancy pill, an oddly formal expression. Quite popular is the i-Pill, a "morning-after" pill, to be taken within 72 hours of the event.

Careful, gentlemen! This is a question better not put. If you ask an Indian woman, particularly an unmarried one, if she takes the pill, you assume that she sleeps around, and in Indian view that likens her to a whore. A married women, too, would probably be rather aghast at such an intimate question. If you insist on asking...

Where can I get condoms/Viagra?	Kāṇḍam/Vaiyegrā kahāñ milegā? कॉंडम/वैयेग्रा कहाँ मिलेगा ?

India is a major manufacturer of generic Viagra, so supply is plentiful and it's usually freely available over the counter. As for condoms, an Indian news magazine once lamented that Indian prostitutes were cheaper than the old rubber hats, but that was certainly an exaggeration. Condoms are inexpensive and these days they come in all kinds of fruity flavors. There's even a *pān*-flavored condom; *pān* being a mix of areca nuts, tobacco, lime paste and other ingredients, the lot being rolled up in a betel leaf and chewed. It's a popular and possibly addictive pastime. Depending on type of preparation, *pān* can have a stimulating effect. We're not sure about the condoms, though.

Is today safe for you?	Tumhāre li(y)e āj surakṣit hai? तुम्हारे लिए आज सुरक्षित है ?
I want you.	Maiñ tum ko cāhtā♂/ cāhtī♀ hūñ. मैं तुम को चाहता/चाहती हूँ ।
How do you want me to do it?	Maiñ tum ko kaise de dūñ? मैं तुम को कैसे दे दूँ ?
I feel so good.	Maiñ bahut khush hūñ. मैं बहुत खुश हूँ ।
Touch me.	Mujhe cun lo. मुझे चुन लो ।
Bite me.	Mujhe kāṭo. मुझे काटो ।
More and more.	Aur aur. और और ।
Do that again.	Aisā dubārā karo. ऐसा दुबारा करो ।
Stronger.	Zabardastī se. ज़बरदस्ती से ।

Softer.	Thoṛā arām se. थोड़ा आराम से।
Faster.	Tezī se. तेज़ी-से।
Slower.	Āhistā-āhistā. आहिस्ता-आहिस्ता।
Deeper.	Aur gahrā. और गहरा।
Did you like that?	Yah tum ko pasand āyā? यह तुम को पसंद आया ?
That was good.	Mazā āyā. मज़ा आया।
That was wonderful.	Yah bahut baṛhiyā thā. यह बहुत बढ़िया था।
I won't ever leave you.	Maiñ tum ko kabhī nahīñ choṛ dūñgā ♂/dūñgī ♀. मैं तुम को कभी नहीं छोड़ दूँगा/दूँगी।
I want to stay with you forever.	Mujhe hameshā tumhāre sāth rahnā cāhtā ♂/cāhtī ♀ hūñ. मैं हमेशा तुम्हारे साथ रहना चाहता/चाती हूँ।
One more time?	Ek bār aur? एक बार और ?
Shall we sleep now?	Ab so jāeñ? अब सो जाएं ?
I'll make you sleep/put you to bed.	Maiñ tum ko sulāūñgā ♂/sulāūñgī ♀. मैं तुम को सुलाऊँगा/सुलाऊँगी।

The Other Side 14

Will you marry me? Mujh se shādī karoge ♂/ karogī ♀?
मुझ से शादी करोगे/करोगी ?

Yes, let's get married. Hāñ, shādī kar leñ.
हाँ, शादी कर लें ।

No, not yet. Nahīñ, abhī nahīñ.
नहीं, अभी नहीं ।

Our relationship will last forever. Hamārā rishtā amar rahegā.
हमारा रिश्ता अमर रहेगा ।

In Hindu thought, ideal married couples were also married in past lives and will be married again in future lives. This type of eternal relationship is called **janam-janam kā rishtā** = relationship through all births/incarnations.

I want to be your wife. Maiñ tumhārī bīvī bannī cāhtī hūñ.
मैं तुम्हारी बीवी बननी चाहती हूँ ।

I want to be your husband. Maiñ tumhārā pati bannā cāhtā hūñ.
मैं तुम्हारा पति बनना चाहता हूँ ।

Will you come to America/ Australia/Europe with me? Mere sāth *America*/*Australia*/ *Europe* caloge ♂/calogī ♀?
मेरे साथ अमेरीका/आस्ट्रेलिया/ यूरोप चलोगे/चलोगी ?

I want to stay in India.	Maiñ Bhārat meñ rahnā cahtā♂/cāhtī♀ hūñ. मैं भारत में रहना चाहता/चाहती हूँ।
I don't want to get married yet.	Is samay mujhe shādī nahīñ karnī cāhi(y)e. इस समय मुझे शादी नहीं करनी चाहिए।
I don't want to get engaged yet.	Is samay mujhe maṅgnī nahīñ karnī cāhi(y)e. इस समय मुझे मँगनी नहीं करनी चाहिए।
I don't even want to think about marriage yet.	Is samay mujhe shādī ke bāre meñ socnā tak nahīñ cāhi(y)e. इस समय मुझे शादी के बारे में सोचना तक नहीं चाहिए।
I love you but I can't marry you.	Mujhe tum se pyār ho gayā, lekin maiñ tum se shādī nahīñ kar sakūñgā♂/ sakūñgī♀. मुझे तुम से प्यार हो गया, लेकिन मैं तुम से शादी नहीं कर सकूँगा/ सकूँगी।
My parents have selected a husband/wife for me.	Mere māñ–bāp ne mere li(y)e ek pati/bīvī ko cun liyā hai. मेरे माँ-बाप ने मेरे लिए एक पति/ बीवी को चुन लिया है।

Note: Most marriages in India are arranged by the parents. Usually, people marry within their own religious community: Hindu, Muslim, Sikh, Christian etc. In addition, Hindus tend to marry within their own caste. So far, few people dare break the mold and opt for "love marriages" crossing caste or community lines. Most Indians view love matches with suspicion.

I'm already married. Merī shādī ho cukī hai.
मेरी शादी हो चुकी है।

I'm already engaged. Merī maṅgnī ho cukī hai.
मेरी मँगनी हो चुकी है।

I need time to think. Mujhe socne ke liye vaḵt cāhi(y)e.
मुझे सोचने के लिए वक़्त चाहिए।

This is so sudden. Yah kāfī jaldī hai.
यह काफ़ी जल्दी है।

We must think about this. Ham ko us ke bāre meñ socnā cāhi(y)e.
हम को उस के बारे में सोचना चाहिए।

You don't love me anymore, do you? Tum ko mujh se pyār nahīñ rahā, hai ki?
तुम को मुझ से प्यार नहीं रहा, है कि?

Do you have another girlfriend?	Tumhāre pās koī dūsrī *girlfriend* hai? तुम्हारे पास कोई दूसरी गर्लफ़्रेंड है ?
Do you have another boyfriend?	Tumhāre pās koī dūsrā *boyfriend* hai? तुम्हारे पास कोई दूसरा बोयफ़्रेंड है ?
Let's not see each other gain.	Phir se nahīñ mileñ. फिर से नहीं मिलें ।
I can't see you anymore.	Tum se phir se mil nahīñ sakūñgā♂/sakūñgī♀. तुम से फिर से मिल नहीं सकूँगा/सकूँगी ।
I don't want to see you anymore.	Tum se phir se nahīñ milnā cāhi(y)e. तुम से फिर से नहीं मिलना चाहिए ।
I have another girlfriend/ boyfriend.	Mere pās ek dusrī *girlfriend*/ dūsrā *boyfriend* hai. मेरे पास एक दूसरी गर्लफ़्रेंड/दूसरा बोयफ़्रेंड है ।
I'm not interested in you anymore.	Tum meñ merā koī shauk̲ nahīñ rahā. तुम में मेरा कोई शौक़ नहीं रहा ।
I'm not good for you.	Maiñ tumhāre♂/tumhāri♀ lāyak nahīñ. मैं तुम्हारे/तुम्हारी लायक़ नहीं ।
Forget about me.	Mujhe bhūlā do! मुझे भूला दो !
I'm sorry it didn't work out.	Maiñ dukhī hūñ ki ham saphal nahīñ rahe. मैं दुःखी हूँ कि हम सफल नहीं रहे ।

It's all over.	Sab <u>kh</u>atam (ho gayā). सब ख़तम (हो गया) ।
I won't call you anymore.	Maiñ tum ko āge nahīñ fon karūñgā♂/karūñgī♀. मैं तुम को आगे नहीं फ़ोन करूँगा/करूँगी ।
Don't call me again.	Āindā mujhe fon na karnā. आइंदा मुझे फ़ोन न करना ।
Let it be!	Rahne do! रहने दो !
I'm sorry, I haven't been a good girlfriend/boyfriend.	Mujhe afsos hai ki maiñ acchā *boyfriend*/acchī *girlfriend* nahīñ thā♂/thī♀. मुझे अफ़सोस है कि मैं अच्छा बोयफ़्रेंड/अच्छी गर्लफ़्रेंड नहीं था/थी ।
It's all my fault.	Sab merī galtī hai. सब मेरी ग़लती है ।
Don't be angry.	Nārāz mat ho. नाराज़ मत हो ।
Can't we start again?	Dubārā shuruāt kar leñ? दुबारा शुरुआत कर लें ?
I'm serious about you.	Maiñ *serious* hūñ tumhāre bāre meñ. मैं सीरीयस हूँ तुम्हारे बारे में ।
I can't live without you.	Tumhāre binā maiñ rah nahīñ saktā♂/saktī♀. तुम्हारे बिना मैं रह नहीं सकता/सकती ।

Understand my feelings.	Mere jazbāt samjho. मेरे जज़बात समझो।
I'll miss you.	Maiñ tum ko *miss* karūñgā♂/karūñgī♀. मैं तुम को मिस करूँगा/करूँगी।

Note: If you want to be more formal, say **Mujhe tumhārī zarūrat mahsūs hogā** = "I'll realize the need for you."

I'll never forget you.	Maiñ tum ko kabhī nahīñ bhūlūñgā♂/bhūlūñgī♀. मैं तुम को कभी नहीं भूलूँगा/भूलूँगी।
I'm so happy to have known you.	Tum se milne se bahut khushī huī. तुम से मिलने से बहुत खुशी हुई।
Remember me sometimes.	Mujhe kabhī yād kiyā karo. मुझे कभी याद किया करो।
I'll remember this day forever.	Āj kā din mujhe hameshā yād rahegā. आज का दिन मुझे हमेशा याद रहेगा।
Can we still be friends?	Ham dost hī rah sakeñge? हम दोस्त ही रह सकेंगे ?
Be happy with her/him.	Unke sāth khush raho. उनके साथ खुश रहो।
I'll always think of you.	Maiñ hameshā tumhārī yād karūñgā♂/karūñgī♀. मैं हमेशा तुम्हारी याद करूँगा/करूँगी।
I'll always love you.	Maiñ tum ko hameshā pyār karūñgā♂/karūñgī♀. मैं तुम को हमेशा प्यार करूँगा/करूँगी।